You're Approved!

The Real Deal About Getting a Mortgage And Buying a Home

You're Approved!

The Real Deal About Getting a
Mortgage And Buying a Home

By: Lynn Richardson and Lori Jones Gibbs

Requests for permission and other inquiries should be addressed to the publisher:

Publisher Name: Yes Enterprises, LLC.
Publisher Address: 6409 Fayetteville Road Suite 120-141
Publisher City, State: Durham, NC 27713
Publisher Phone: 888.LORI234 (888.567.4234)
Publisher Email: lori@yesenterprisesllc.com
Publisher Website: www.yesenterprisesllc.com

ISBN 13:   978-0-9819749-0-3

Cover Designed by: Beth Greene
Book Designed by: 1st Choice Communications Group

Additional Contact: Lynn Richardson Enterprises, Inc
                         PO Box 2815 Country Club Hills, IL 60478
Website: www.lynnrichardson.com
Email: dreamscometrue@lynnrichardson.com
Phone: 888.LYNN123 (888.596.6123)

Your Everyday Success

ADDITIONAL BOOKS BY LYNN RICHARDSON

Living Check to Monday: The Real Deal About Money, Credit and Financial Security

Living Beyond Check to Monday: A Spiritual Path to Wealth and Prosperity

FORTHCOMING BOOK BY LORI JONES GIBBS

Yes, I Would Marry Him Again

FORTHCOMING BOOK BY YES ENTERPRISES, LLC

Yes, Your Finances Can Recover: Money Tips to Help You in Any Economy

ACKNOWLEDGMENTS

First, I must say thank you to the true Author of this book, the One I serve, and the Source through which all blessings flow. . . God. Most of what is shared in this work is from personal life experience, and I truly thank God for blessing me with the tests to share this testimony.

I thank my husband, Demietrius, and my daughters, Cydney, Taylor and Kennedy, for their love and support and for being the inspiration for my earthly aspirations.

I thank Grandma Bea, who raised me, and who showed me undying love and support from infancy and who always made me feel as if I could conquer the world.

I thank my parents who gave me life and who passed on the gifts of gab and curiosity (mom) and the gifts of discernment and strategy (dad).

I thank my second mom, Diane Holda, my Sorors (especially Lori, Deadra, Sonya and Kemba), my business partners, colleagues, friends, and spiritual advisors for all of your kind words, thoughts, prayers and support.

This book is dedicated to Melody Spann Cooper, Latrice Spann Levitt, and the entire WVON 1690 family.

LYNN RICHARDSON

*T*hank you to God, my provider and sustainer.

I thank my husband Kenneth, my source of strength, for always being there for me and our families.

To my daughters, Claudia and Tanisa, and my son Kenneth Jr....I finally did it! Thanks for your love, encouragement and persistence.

To my parents, Henry and Sarah Jones, thank you for life, love and support and for always caring.

To my co-author, sister-friend, Soror, and yes, young'n...this is the first of several books we will author together. Thank you, you're the best!

A special Thanks to Mudy Stone for your editorial support; love you much.

To all who contributed, edited and supported this effort, I give THANKS.

LORI JONES GIBBS

Table of Contents

Table of Contents

Foreword

*I*t's about 660 miles from Bridgeport, Connecticut to Topsail Island on the coast of North Carolina. Making the trip takes about eleven and a half hours by car. It's a long drive, but you can do it in a day. Making the economic journey from public housing in Bridgeport's P.T. Barnum Apartments to a vacation home on Topsail is another story entirely.

We all dream of a bright financial future, of building wealth and opening the door to opportunity for ourselves and for our families. I know I did as I grew up in a small North Carolina town in a family with limited personal resources. My parents taught me the value of hard work as the first step of achieving that dream. It may come easy to some, but most people would need a roadmap to help them plot their journey. You're holding one now. It's a step-by-step guide to realizing the American dream of home ownership and that is an important milestone as you make your own journey to economic well being.

That was true for my college classmate, Kenny Gibbs, and his wife, Lori. Here were two kids from the Bridgeport projects who got engaged after college and needed a place to live. Lori tells their story in *Yes, You're Approved.* As someone just starting out in the mortgage business, she says, "In those days, I knew just enough to be dangerous," but the initial decisions she made with Kenny about home ownership helped start them on the road to prosperity and weekends at their vacation home on the North Carolina shore.

Lori would probably acknowledge modestly that she knows a lot more today about housing and mortgages than she did as a first-time buyer. You learn a lot during nearly 30 years in an industry. If you're lucky, you also meet people with similar knowledge and experience who share your commitment to making home ownership a reality for all who are ready - people like Lynn Richardson, who, before the age of 30, became an urban media and real estate phenomenon by helping aspiring families overcome financial roadblocks to achieve the dream of homeownership.

As co-authors, Lynn and Lori make a terrific combination. Accomplished, innovative and passionate about what they do, they both have the ability to translate the often mystifying process of buying a house into words and concepts we all can understand. In doing so, they give their readers the information they need to feel comfortable when making what is probably the largest investment of their lives.

That's quite an accomplishment at a time when feeling comfortable isn't exactly the first thing that comes to mind when thinking about real estate transactions. Over the past few years, home prices have plunged and foreclosures have soared, and the turmoil in housing is still not over. But that's no reason to shy away from home ownership. Ironically, the very challenges facing today's mortgage market are now creating opportunities for home buyers who understand what to look for and what to avoid in getting a mortgage, buying a home and then being able to stay in that home.

Now that the housing bubble has burst, the inventory of homes on the market at affordable prices is a buyer's delight. Low interest rates and government incentives make the case for buying now even more compelling. The days of no-money down, interest-only-option ARMs, and other exotic mortgage products that made getting a mortgage easy, but helped create the mortgage crisis, are over. But safe, secure mortgage options are still available to qualified first-time, move-up, and low-to-moderate-income buyers.

Lynn and Lori tell you what these options are and how to take advantage of them so you, too, can hear the words, *"Yes, You're Approved."* There's nothing like unlocking the door and walking into a home of your own for the first time, and there's nothing better than knowing what to do to KEEP the home you already have and to pass on a legacy to future generations.

You're about to take the first step.

Have a wonderful journey.

James H. Speed, Jr.

President and Chief Executive Officer,
North Carolina Mutual Life Insurance Company

Introduction

"*L*ead me into a career that will allow me to help people, control my schedule, and earn a salary commensurate with my work ethic." That was my prayer.

The mortgage industry was the answer.

That was over twelve years ago. Back then, the industry was different. Aspiring homebuyers actually had to document their ability to obtain a mortgage with paystubs, W-2 forms, bank statements, and tax returns. Loan professionals actually had to **know** how to put a loan file together, qualify a potential homebuyer and calculate mortgage insurance – all by hand and without the help of fancy computer programs. Aspiring homebuyers applied for mortgages and were given, in most cases, one of three options – Conventional, Federal Housing Administration (FHA), and Veteran's Administration (VA).

And then, right after the Y2K craze was over, the industry changed.

Loan officers no longer had to calculate anything by hand, or even figure out the details of a good faith estimate. Computers did it for them. This was the equivalent of giving a first grader a calculator and expecting him to really understand why one plus one equals two.

Homeseekers were able to go to the mortgage drive-through

window and order a 30-year, interest-only, stated-income loan with extra points and a prepayment penalty on the side – in exchange for little or no documentation – and drive off with their fast-food mortgages and dreams into la-la land.

And then came the nightmare on Dream Street -- the biggest housing crisis in the history of the world happened.

Interest rates increased. Homeowners walked away. Mortgage companies closed like there was no tomorrow. And the entire economy fell prey to the after effects of what was supposed to be the American Dream.

And yet, it's still a great time to buy a home. That's right. . . within your means. . . with appropriate knowledge and education. . . safely and securely.

Here's to a full course meal and the real deal about obtaining your piece of the American Dream.

Lynn Richardson

The Mortgage Guru

hy?

Because you can.

I am often asked about my passion for homeownership. It's simple. Homeownership is the foundation for wealth creation – especially in today's market – because owning a home, safely and securely, provides you with certain rights and privileges, like deducting the interest on your mortgage loan and reducing your taxable income.

The story below is why homeownership is my passion.

Twenty seven years ago, a couple got engaged and decided it was time for them to find a place to live. It was the young lady's task to find them a place. She found a co-op, and they went to a lender and inquired about getting a loan to make the purchase. Their loan was denied!!! The young lady was upset about being turned down. She was upset because she and her fiancé were first generation college graduates, they were requesting a $5,000.00 loan and they were told "NO!" She and her fiancé realized it would cost them $450.00 per month in 1980 to live in a one bedroom apartment without appliances or utilities.

So what did they do? They made it a point to learn more about their options, and they returned to the same lender a month and a half later. This time they were knowledgeable about mortgage insurance and how it helps individuals purchase homes with low down payments. The lender approved their loan, and they purchased their first home... a 3-bedroom, 1 bath colonial. Five years later they sold that home and earned a 100% profit in equity dollars. They took some of the profit and bought their first investment property (a three-unit building for which their mortgage payment was $620.00. They charged $400.00 rent per unit per month. You do the math. They realized a $580.00 monthly profit). In the meantime, they were building a new 4 bedroom, 2½ bath, one-car garage home for themselves. Seven years later they sold that home, earned a 50% increase in equity dollars and purchased the home they now live in — five bedrooms, 2 ½ baths with a two-car garage. While they were on this wealth building journey, the couple was also able to acquire other investment properties and a second home at the beach.

Homeownership has enabled them to invest in the stock market. It allowed the husband to start his own business, and it would have enabled them to pay for their children's college education (had they not earned full scholarships).

These two kids, who grew up in public housing learned how to leverage other people's money (credit), firmly believe that homeownership has put them in a comfortable financial position.

I know how they feel because it's the wealth journey that I've made along with my husband. We have always believed that if we could make that journey, so can others like us. Others like you — like the people you know and see every day.

"Yes, You're Approved!" is more than a book — it's a toolkit that will help you achieve and maintain your dream of homeownership . . . safely and securely.

Lori Jones Gibbs

The People's Guru

PART ONE

The Mortgage Approval Process

Chapter One

**Before You Apply for a Mortgage –
Be in the Know**

Chapter One

Before You Apply for a Mortgage – Be in the Know

*P*ersonal finance experts warn that you must have perfect credit and a twenty percent downpayment to get approved for a mortgage as a result of the housing crisis. Nothing could be further from the truth! Certainly, they don't mean any harm. While well-intentioned, they simply don't have the inside knowledge about the mortgage industry to demystify the mortgage and homebuying process and understand the intricate options available to today's homeowners and homebuyers.

In fact, a great number of industry insiders do not truly understand the art of getting the single parent, recent college graduate, young aspiring couple, or other atypical buyer approved for a mortgage loan. So please follow these steps before you apply for a mortgage and before you shop for a home; therefore, you will minimize unnecessary frustration during the homebuying process.

1. **Attend a Homebuyer Education Course**

   a. Enroll in a homebuyer education course in order to fully understand the mortgage and homebuying process from the inside out.

b. Contact any HUD approved not-profit housing counseling agency in your community to get assistance with credit and debt counseling (http://www.hud.gov/offices/hsg/sfh/hcc/hcs.cfm).

2. **Pay Your Past Due Collections**

   a. Organize your records and pay all collections, charge-offs, and judgments.

   b. Pay off the smaller bills first and make arrangements to pay the larger bills in installments.

   c. If you make a payment plan on the larger collections and stick to that plan for at least twelve months, the underwriter <u>may</u> approve your loan even if you are unable to pay the debt in full. However, you should make every attempt to pay all collections in full.

   d. Get all payment arrangements in writing.

   e. Get paid-in-full letters for all debts that are satisfied and keep copies for your lender.

   f. Obtain a <u>RELEASE/SATISFACTION OF JUDGMENT</u> for all judgments that are satisfied. (Also, if a judgment was erroneously entered against you and/or if the plaintiff is willing, request that the judgment be vacated. This will prevent the judgment from appearing on your credit report.)

   g. <u>If you are paying off these debts before closing,</u> pay via money order, western union, money gram, or cashier's check and save the receipt for your records. Also, get a letter from the creditor indicating that your account has been satisfied or settled and send a copy to your lender as well.

3. **Pay Your Current Bills on Time**

    a. Pay all current bills on time each and every month, with a special focus on those creditors who report to the credit bureaus.

    b. Pay all bills even if they are not reported, since creditors may decide to report outstanding debts (for example medical bills and utilities) to the credit bureau in the event they are not paid on time). This is known in the industry as negative or adverse credit reporting.

    c. Pay your bills with a check, money order, or other electronic method that can be verified in the event there is a dispute regarding your payment history.

4. **Assess Your Student Loans**

    a. If you have student loans, consider consolidating them into a lower payment and request a deferment/forbearance if you are unable to pay them now.

    b. Student loans that remain in deferment status for at least one year beyond your closing date may not be counted in your debt-to-income ratio during the mortgage approval process, thus enabling you to obtain a mortgage. However; it's a good idea to plan for the payment in the future.

c. If you have questions about consolidating your student loans, contact the Direct Loan Servicing Center: (800) 848-0979 – http://loanconsolidation.ed.gov/.

d. Contact Sallie Mae: (800) 272-5543 – www.salliemae.com.

5. **Contact all three credit reporting agencies to make sure accounts are reported accurately. You are entitled to one free credit report per year: www.annualcreditreport.com.**

a. Request all three credit reports: www.experian.com; www.equifax.com; www.transunion.com.

b. Dispute all incorrect information and be prepared to submit documentation (pay off letters, bankruptcy discharge papers, etc.) to validate your dispute. See the credit dispute section on the form in the reference section of this book named "Obtain a Copy of Your Credit Report."

6. **Keep the money that is being saved for the down payment in an account, untouched, until your mortgage is approved.**

a. Even if it's only $100 per pay period, the underwriter will look favorably upon your mortgage application if a consistent savings plan is established.

b. Be creative! Your tax refund, security deposit, 401k savings, and many other sources may be tapped as a source of down payment.

7. **DON'T GIVE UP**

    a. If you follow these steps, you WILL BECOME A HOME OWNER in due time!

    b. Remember, time will pass whether or not you follow the above outlined components of the Mortgage Approval Plan (MAP) – the question you have to ask yourself is "Where do I want to be when the time passes?" Hopefully, your answer is, "In my new home!"

Chapter Two

Documents Required During the Mortgage Application Process – Paperwork Is a Reality

Chapter Two

Documents Required During the Mortgage Application Process – Paperwork Is a Reality

*O*ne of the most frustrating things about the mortgage application process is the never-ending requests from your lender to provide "conditions," or additional documentation, to explain or enhance what you already submitted. This chapter will help you provide a complete application for even the most difficult loan. The rule of thumb is to provide as much documentation as possible so your file will be well organized and approvable after the first review. When you leave out important information, it raises additional questions and makes it harder to approve your loan in the end.

Also, accept the fact that you may get frustrated, bite your nails, cry, pray, or whatever you do when the pressure is on. It's all part of the process. But remember, in the end, you will have your new home!

1. **Paystubs**

    a. Provide paystubs for one full month. If you get paid every week, provide four paystubs. If you get paid every other week, provide two. If you get paid once per month, provide two paystubs so the lender will have something to compare to.

b. If there are any drastic changes to your paycheck, please explain in writing. For example, if you get paid every week and one paycheck is significantly less than the others, explain this in writing (time off work; bonus received, overtime, etc.)

c. Underwriters will scrutinize your paycheck for deductions that you may have failed to disclose during the application process (credit union loan payments; garnishments; child support deductions; union dues, etc.) so be up front about any and all debts you are responsible for paying.

2. **Other Proof of Income**

   a. Social Security

      i. Provide a copy of the Social Security Awards Letter, proof that it has been received for the past three months, and proof that it will continue for at least the next three years.

      ii. If the social security is for a child or dependent and you are the payee, you must provide a copy of the person's birth certificate in order to substantiate whether or not the social security will continue for the next three years.

      iii. If the social security is for someone who has a disability, you must provide proof that the disability is expected to continue for the next three years (get a letter from a physician).

b. Pension / Retirement / Veteran's Income

c. Interest Income

d. Foster Care/Adoption Income (provide a letter from the case worker and proof that the income will continue for at least three years)

3. **Bank Statements and Evidence of Funds to Close**

a. Provide bank statements for at least two months.

b. There should be no non-sufficient funds (NSF) fees (you know, bounced check or overdraft fees) on any bank statements. This is a sign that you may not be ready to handle the responsibility of a mortgage.

c. Provide all pages of your bank statements and make sure you provide your saving statements as well.

d. Provide 401(k) statements, certificates of deposit, mutual funds, or any assets that you wish to have considered in determining your discipline and/or ability to get approved for a mortgage.

e. Explain any large deposits and provide proof. For example, if you received a tax refund, provide a copy of the check or your tax refund documentation. Large deposits that cannot be explained will not be considered as available cash for closing. The reason for this is the lender wants to make sure you are not borrowing money (it's okay to borrow from a 401(k) or other retirement account in most cases) and therefore putting yourself in more debt.

f. Last two years W-2 forms and tax returns. If you changed jobs, provide all W-2s and write a letter indicating the timeline of your job history – do not leave any time gaps. You may also submit a resume. The underwriter wants to know that you have a consistent employment history, as well as reasonable evidence that you will have income for the next three years.

If you are a recent college graduate and do not have two years of employment, you can still get approved for a mortgage if you have the following:

i. A copy of your college transcript, your degree and your first paystub on your new job in your field of study.

ii. Less than a four-year degree and at least one year of work history in your field of study.

4. **Housing Payment History:**

a. Name, Address & Phone # of Landlord; or

b. Last twelve cancelled mortgage/rent checks; or

c. Letter from your landlord indicating the date you began renting and whether or not you have paid your rent on time for the past twelve months or provide copies of twelve months cancelled rental payment checks; or

d. In the event you have not paid rent, a letter indicating that you have been living at home "rent free." In this instance, your credit, down payment and other application details must compensate substantially for the fact that you do not have any housing payment history.

5. **Non-Traditional Credit**

    a. If you do not have any established credit on your credit report, submit three or four references in the form of a letter from your creditor (utilities, insurance payments, cell phone, daycare payments, tuition, etc.) — see "Forms You Can Use" in Part Six; or

    b. Submit a twelve-month payment history for each credit reference if the creditor is unable or unwilling to provide a letter.

6. **Letter of Explanation**

    a. If you have any collections, judgments, late payments or bankruptcies, you must submit a letter of explanation to your lender (see "Forms You Can Use" in Part Six).

    b. The letter of explanation should explain the following for each derogatory item:

        i.   Why the bad/poor credit occurred;

        ii. What you have learned; and

        iii. How you will do better in the future.

7. **Bankruptcy Papers**

    a. Provide all pages of all filing and discharge papers.

    b. See the next chapter for additional documents and steps for Post-Bankruptcy applicants.

8. **Additional Approval Documentation for High Debt Ratios**

The housing debt ratio is

$$\frac{\text{PITI (Principal Interest Taxes Insurance)} + \text{Assessments}}{\text{Your Gross Monthly Income}}$$

The total debt ratio is

$$\frac{\text{PITI} + \text{Assessments} + \text{all other debt (credit cards, loans, etc)}}{\text{Your Gross Monthly Income}}$$

Typically, your housing ratio cannot be higher than 31% and your total debt ratio cannot be higher than 43%. Some programs have higher and/or lower debt ratio guidelines. The following factors can help you qualify for a mortgage in the event your debt ratio is too high.

a. **Other Peoples' Debt**: If you co-signed for someone and that person pays the bill and you do NOT want this debt to be included in your debt ratio when qualifying for a mortgage, you need to provide the following:

   i. Twelve consecutive cancelled checks documenting one year of timely payments from the other person's bank account (if it is a joint bank account with you, it won't work!)

   ii. Any additional documentation that validates that the other person is paying the bill (for example, repair bills for the car, receipts and signatures of the other party, etc.)

b. **Less than Ten Months**: For most loan programs, installment debts (car notes, student loans, etc.) with less than ten months to completion do not have to be included in your debt ratio. This is not the case for revolving debts (credit cards, charge accounts, etc.)

c. **Overtime and other Income**: If you have a two-year history of overtime, bonuses, or income from a second job, this income can help you qualify for a home. In most cases, you must be able to document this income source for the previous two years, and your lender will take a 24-month average. So if you earned $5,000 in overtime last year and $3,000 in overtime the year before, the following calculation shows the additional monthly income that can be used to help you qualify:

($5,000 + $3000) divided by 24 months = $250 additional monthly income to help you qualify

d. **Taxes and Insurance**: Did your lender overestimate the monthly taxes and insurance for your home? Ask your lender to make sure your payment estimate is based on accurate information and provide a current real estate tax bill, home owners insurance quote, or other documentation to support your application.

e. **Assessments Minus Utilities**: If you will pay assessments for the purchase of a condominium or townhome, then **the portion of your assessments that cover utilities** (electric, heat, water, cable) **SHOULD NOT** be included in your debt ratio calculation. Obtain a budget or other documentation from the homeowner's association that clearly outlines the portion of the previous year's assessment payments that were allocated to utilities.

Chapter Three

**Getting Approved for a Mortgage after
a Bankruptcy – Yes You Can**

Chapter Three

Getting Approved for a Mortgage after a Bankruptcy – Yes You Can

M any believe that buying a home after a bankruptcy is impossible. This is NOT TRUE! In fact, there are countless instances where those who file bankruptcy and then rebuild their credit responsibly obtain mortgages with market interest rates quicker than those who allow bad/poor credit to linger for years. The key is to be armed with correct knowledge.

CHAPTER 13 APPLICANTS

IF AT LEAST ONE YEAR HAS ELAPSED SINCE THE FILING DATE OF YOUR CHAPTER 13 BANKRUPTCY, please follow all the steps outlined in the chapter entitled "Before You Apply for a Mortgage," plus submit to your lender:

1.   Complete Chapter 13 filing papers, plus Chapter 13 payment history from the Bankruptcy Trustee's Office.

2.   Permission (in writing) from the Bankruptcy Trustee to enter into a mortgage transaction. Your attorney can help you obtain this letter or you may request it directly from your Bankruptcy Trustee.

IF LESS THAN ONE YEAR HAS ELAPSED SINCE THE FILING DATE OF YOUR CHAPTER 13 BANKRUPTCY, you must wait until the one-year anniversary of your filing date to apply for a mortgage.

1. Pay all of your bills and trustee payments on time during this period.

2. After your one-year anniversary, obtain permission to enter into a mortgage transaction from the Bankruptcy Trustee and a printout of your bankruptcy payment history, and submit this to your lender along with other documents requested.

CHAPTER 7 APPLICANTS

IF AT LEAST TWO YEARS HAVE ELAPSED SINCE YOUR DISCHARGE DATE, and you have been following the steps outlined in the chapter entitled "Before You Apply for a Mortgage," you may be eligible for a mortgage. Contact your lender and be prepared to submit your Chapter 7 Filing and Discharge papers, plus the items in Section 3 below.

IF LESS THAN TWO YEARS HAVE ELAPSED SINCE YOUR DISCHARGE DATE, in most cases, you must wait until your two-year anniversary to apply for a mortgage, unless you can document that the reason for bankruptcy was beyond your control (for example, loss of income due to divorce, death, down-sizing, or medical illness).

GENERAL RULE FOR ALL POST-BANKRUPTCY HOME SEEKERS

1. Pay all of your bills on time for the 24-month period preceding your mortgage application. Underwriters will not look favorably at your loan if you pay bills late after a

bankruptcy. Beware of medical collections. If a bill comes in the mail, reconcile with your insurance provider, pay it if you can, or make arrangements with the service provider IMMEDIATELY before it goes to collection. One small dental collection for one little tooth could be the roadblock that keeps you from achieving your dream.

2. Live far below your means so it will be easier to restore your credit.

3. Do not accept too many new credit offers. Get one or two credit cards, keep the balances down to less than 40 percent of the credit limit, and pay at least twice the minimum payment on time, before the due date, each month. It is important to pay before the due date. When you pay after the due date, you may be subject to a higher interest rate, or a decrease in your credit limit, which can damage your credit rating and future opportunities to obtain credit.

4. Avoid getting a car note if at all possible. This is one of the first offers you will receive after filing for bankruptcy. Instead, save and attempt to buy a car with cash, or if you must get a car note, obtain a pre-driven vehicle with low miles in order to keep the price and financing costs down.

5. Immediately contact all three credit bureaus to ensure that accounts included in bankruptcy are removed from or properly noted on your credit report.

Chapter Four

The Mortgage Approval Process Step by Step – A Safe, Secure Way to Homeownership

Chapter Four

The Mortgage Approval Process Step by Step – a Safe, Secure Way to Homeownership

PREAPPROVAL vs. PREQUALIFICATION

*W*hat's the difference? A prequalification typically means the lender has looked at your credit and provided you with a preliminary estimate of your buying power without verifying your paystubs, bank statements and other supporting information.

A preapproval, on the other hand, typically means the lender has looked at your credit and provided you with an underwriter's approval and predetermination of your buying power after having reviewed your credit report and all supporting documentation (paystubs, bank statements, tax papers, letters of explanation, etc.).

We highly recommend that you get preapproved for a mortgage before you begin shopping for a home. Even if you have good credit, one incorrect assumption or a miscalculation of income could be the cause of your loan getting denied. If this happens AFTER you have found a home and paid for an appraisal, home inspection and other items, quite naturally you will be frustrated and devastated. Avoid this headache and get preapproved for your mortgage loan before you start looking for a home.

MORTGAGE PREAPPROVAL PROCESS – BEFORE YOU FIND YOUR HOME

1. **Submit any and all documentation that may be required of you as soon as possible as noted in Chapter Two: "Documents Required During the Mortgage Application Process."** Make sure your documents are legible and complete. If, for example, you need to send a bank statement, make sure you send all pages of the bank statement. If you do not have a bank statement at home, get a 60-day print-out from the teller and make sure it is STAMPED AND SIGNED by a bank employee.

2. **Keep all the paperwork that you submitted with your loan application in a convenient location**. You may want to keep these items with you at work in case you need to re-submit a particular item. In addition, keep your current and future paystubs and bank statements handy. Your lender may request them at a later date.

3. **Once your loan is preapproved, your lender will provide a Preapproval Letter or Conditional Loan Commitment**. Your interest rate cannot be guaranteed at this time because a property address is required in order for an interest rate to be locked. So remember, if the rates change before you find a home, this could affect the amount of your loan approval. For example, if at the time of your approval your lender estimates your monthly mortgage payment at an interest rate of 6%, then your approval will be based on this payment at this interest rate. If, however, you find a home months later and the interest rate at that time is 7%, then the payment will be higher. You may not be able to qualify. So it is very important to stay abreast of market rates while you are

shopping for your new home.

4. **Continue to pay all of your bills on time. DO NOT apply for or accept any new credit during the mortgage process.** Some insurance companies may pull your credit report to determine your qualification for premium homeowner's insurance rates. Whatever decision your insurance agent makes, this will not reflect negatively on your mortgage application. In addition, be sure to manage your checking account wisely. Underwriters do not want to see returned checks on your bank statement.

5. **Continue to save for your down payment** and keep the money that will be used for closing in a checking or savings account. *Also, fax or mail new paystubs and bank statements to your lender every 4 weeks until you close. This will allow the lender to assess any significant changes in your file and address them in a timely manner.*

6. **Work with your real estate professional to find a property in your price range.**

7. **Secure an attorney or title company to represent you at closing.**

MORTGAGE APPROVAL PROCESS – AFTER YOU FIND YOUR HOME

1. **Work with your real estate professional to make a valid offer on the property.** Remember, if you are asking the seller to pay your closing costs, you should do so at this time.

2. **After your contract has been accepted, submit your**

earnest money (down payment) to your real estate professional in a timely fashion. This is customarily $1,000, or one percent of the sales price (applied to your down payment). The earnest money should be tendered in the form of a cashier's check or money order for easy verification by the lender.

3. **Within three business days, you should receive a document entitled "Good Faith Estimate."** Now is also the time to lock in your interest rate. The Good Faith Estimate is a comprehensive outline of the terms, interest rate, monthly payment, down payment, and fees associated with your loan. Remember, this is an estimate. The actual day of closing, your homeowner's insurance premium, and actual taxes on the property, among other things, could change one or more figures in your Good Faith Estimate.

4. **Within three business days, you should receive a document entitled "Truth In Lending Disclosure,"** which outlines the terms of your loan. You will see two figures (1) Interest Rate and (2) APR, or Annual Percentage Rate – which is <u>not</u> the same as your interest rate. The APR is a financial term that tells you the <u>cost</u> of your credit, including certain fees. If all is well, you should sign the document and return a copy to your lender acknowledging your acceptance and understanding.

5. **Submit a cashier's check or money order to your lender for your appraisal**. You may also be able to provide a credit or debit card or tender the payment directly to the appraiser – in that case, you will need a cashier's check or money order made payable to the appraiser. Your appraisal will be ordered by the lender after payment is secured. If

you are purchasing a multi-unit or commercial property, or if you are obtaining an FHA or VA loan, the fee for your appraisal may be higher.

6.   **Contact your attorney** to let him/her know when your anticipated closing will take place.

7.   **Work very closely with the loan processor to ensure that you have submitted all required documentation for your mortgage application.** Send any updated paystubs and bank statements as you receive them.

8.   **If you will receive a gift from a relative as a source of funds to close, the transfer of the gift from the donor to you must be documented as follows:** The donor must withdraw the money from his/her bank account and provide the lender with a copy of the bank statement or withdrawal slip showing that the money has been withdrawn. You must deposit the funds into your account and provide the lender with a copy of your bank statement showing that the funds have been deposited. Remember, anytime you get a 60-day printout of your account from your bank, make sure it is **stamped and signed** by a bank representative. **Or, if you do not deposit the funds, get a cashier's check from the donor to you, send your lender a copy of the cashier's check, and bring that same cashier's check to closing with you.**

9.   **Contact your insurance company as soon as possible to get a quote for homeowner's insurance.** Your insurance agent will need specific information about your property, so make sure you get a Multiple Listing Service (MLS) sheet from your real estate professional or information about the

property from your builder. <u>IN MOST CASES, YOU WILL NEED TO SUBMIT PAYMENT TO YOUR INSURANCE AGENT FOR THE FIRST YEAR'S PREMIUM IN ADVANCE, APPROXIMATELY 5 DAYS BEFORE CLOSING and fax proof of payment to your lender.</u> This amount will be determined by the purchase price, location, and type of property you are purchasing. Do not forget to bring your proof of insurance to closing.

10. **Once all of your documents have been submitted and verified, you will receive a Conditional Loan Commitment.** Pay close attention to conditions that must be met before closing as well as those conditions that must be met at the closing.

11. **Confirm the final amount you need to bring to closing with your attorney**. In most cases, your attorney should have figures available the day before or the day of closing (usually later in the day). Don't worry – if you bring too much money, the title/settlement agent will issue you a refund in the form of a cashier's check before you leave the closing.

12. **Your closing funds should be in the form of a CASHIER'S CHECK, from you, and made payable to you (your name as indicated in the loan papers)**. Cash, personal checks, and money orders are not acceptable forms of payment at real estate closings. **Important: if you are receiving a gift and the gift check was not deposited into your bank account as indicated in #8 above, you must bring the gift cashier's check to the closing even if this means you are bringing too much money. You will be reimbursed at the closing if you have too much money.**

If you do not follow these instructions exactly as they are given, YOU MAY NOT BE ABLE TO CLOSE ON YOUR HOME.

13. **Show up at the closing with a valid state identification card or driver's license**. Please be sure to be on time. If you are married and your spouse has not been approved for the mortgage along with you, he/she MUST attend the closing (also with a valid state ID or driver's license) to sign important documentation.

Chapter Five

**Predatory Lending –
Beware, the Loan Sharks Are out
There!**

Chapter Five

Predatory Lending – Beware, the Loan Sharks Are out There!

P **redatory** lending is the practice of using unfair, deceptive, and abusive tactics in lending money. Unscrupulous lenders in the mortgage and consumer lending industries take advantage of borrowers who are less knowledgeable about lending practices, getting them to agree to loan terms that are not only less than desirable, but also financially damaging. Predatory lenders also target borrowers who are so desperate to obtain loans that they will agree to nearly anything.

Predatory lending does not discriminate and it is not simply focused on those with poor credit. Individuals from all backgrounds, credit grades, income levels and walks of life can be victims of predatory lending. Individuals with low incomes and low credit scores are often targets, as well as women, senior citizens, and minorities.

Many consider payday loans predatory lending. Typically, these short-term loans are offered to individuals without regard to credit. Though these loans are relatively easy to obtain, they are granted at unreasonably high interest rates. In fact, an individual who borrows from a payday loan company may pay more than 100-percent interest over the life of the entire loan. With interest rates so high, many payday loan borrowers find repaying their loans very difficult, and sometimes impossible.

Predatory lending is all too common among unscrupulous mortgage lenders. These mortgage lenders offer loans at very high interest rates, requiring borrowers to agree to terms that are unfair and damaging. For example, a predatory lender may require unfair prepayment penalties (fees for paying your loan early) and/or balloon payments (large lump sum payments). Often, these terms are hidden within very technical language, making it difficult for the borrower to fully understand what he or she is agreeing to.

Another example of predatory lending involves consumer loans that are backed by collateral. These loans often carry extremely high interest rates and require the borrower to offer a house or car as collateral. If the borrower defaults, the lender may take possession of the borrower's property and sell it to repay the loan. If the lender sells the collateral for more than the amount of the loan, the lender may actually make a profit on the defaulted loan.

To avoid falling victim to predatory lending, avoid lenders that advertise guaranteed loan approval. Also, be wary of loans advertised through telemarketers or traveling salespeople. Thoroughly research the lending company you are considering to learn if it has been accused of predatory lending. Read all loan agreements carefully before you sign and make sure there are no blank spaces on your loan document. It is also wise to consult with a lawyer before you sign a loan document.

The Most Important Question to Ask Your Lender IS NOT related to the interest rate!

All too often, eager homebuyers fall prey to the lender who quotes the lowest interest rate. Shopping for the lowest interest rate is like shopping for the lowest gas price: if you keep looking, you can always find a lower one, but it's not necessarily the best quality! In fact, if a lender quotes an interest rate without knowing pertinent information about you and your transaction, you should RUN! Prematurely quoting an interest rate is no different than getting a prescription before your doctor checks your vital signs. It's a recipe for disaster that may lead to a quick financial death.

The following is a list of questions you should ask a lending representative before conducting any business:

1.   How long has the company been in business?

2.   Who is the owner and what is his / her background?

3.   How long have you been practicing as a mortgage professional?

4.   Are you required to be licensed? If yes, may I see your license? If no, under what licensing authority do you practice?

5.   Why did you choose this profession?

6.   Can you please provide the names and phone numbers of 5 customer referrals?

7.   Can you please provide the names and phone numbers of 5 professionals from different companies who can attest to your knowledge, service and professionalism?

8.   What type of loans do you typically recommend to your customers and why?

9. How often do you participate in homebuyer education workshops and seminars?

10. What is the average loan amount you typically originate?

11. How many loans have you personally closed within the past month? Past 6 months? Past year? Can you provide proof?

12. Are you knowledgeable about originating conventional, FHA, and VA loans, and can you help me compare the difference between all three if I qualify?

13. What system do you have in place to service buyers who have credit challenges?

Chapter Six

**Understanding Mortgage Products –
the Good, the Bad and the Ugly**

Chapter Six

Understanding Mortgage Products – the Good, the Bad and the Ugly

With Contributions by Paul Imura

T *he interest-only mortgage is not a good product . . .*

That mortgage product with payment options is predatory. . .

I want the product with the best deal. . .

I want the product that enables me to buy the most house. . .

What product can I use and not report my income and assets?

Whether these statements seem enticing or scary, the truth of the matter is this: each mortgage is designed for a specific purpose – much like prescriptions are designed to treat specific ailments – and every mortgage product is not the right prescription for every consumer.

Here are things to consider when choosing a mortgage product that's right for you:

1. In today's market, 30-year fixed rate mortgages can give you peace-of-mind, which is priceless when times get tough. Our personal belief is that most first-time

homebuyers should get a 30-year Fixed Rate Mortgage. Why? You never know how long you will stay in a home. You can assume your income will grow over time, but it's nice to know your mortgage costs won't go up. With a 30-year mortgage, you are protected against rates going up and this will provide you with tremendous peace of mind.

2. If you know you are going to move in a few years, then a hybrid Adjustable Rate Mortgage (ARM) may be a good idea if the rate is lower than 30-year fixed-rate mortgages. An example of a hybrid ARM is a 5/1 adjustable rate mortgage. The first number represents the fixed period and the second number represents how often the rate can adjust after the fixed period. So the 5/1 hybrid ARM will remain fixed for five years and then may adjust every year up to the maximum amount set for each adjustment period. In addition, government ARMs, like FHA or VA adjustable rate mortgages, generally have favorable adjustment terms and generally provide more payment security than other types of ARMs.

Here is a Checklist for Good Mortgage Products:

✓ Fixed Payment

✓ Amortizing…meaning you build up equity as you make payments

✓ Full documentation (no assumptions regarding income or assets)

✓ Lower Underwriting Ratios (no more than 31% of your gross income towards mortgage costs and no more than 41% of your gross income towards all bills – including the mortgage)   You want to make sure you have money left over for building cash reserves, emergencies, saving and investing, basic living expenses, vacationing, and enjoying life.

If you are a financially disciplined, knowledgeable, and, higher-income home buyer or investor, an interest-only mortgage may be a better product for you. You get the benefit of lower payments, higher tax deductions, and alternative use of principal payments. For example, if the interest-only mortgage payment is $400 less than the regular principal and interest mortgage payment, a disciplined and knowledgeable buyer would use the additional funds to decrease other high interest rate debt, build retirement and savings, or maximize other investment opportunities. It IS NOT a good idea to use the additional funds to purchase a MORE EXPENSIVE home.

One thing to note about the interest-only mortgage is that it was designed and used by commercial banks to extend loans to builders who needed financing to construct homes that they planned to sell in the short-term.   In this instance, the entire mortgage balance would be paid within a short period of time and the builder would maximize its cashflow in the process.

So why is there so much bad mouthing of interest-only mortgages?

It's because this is not the right "prescription" for the average first time homebuyer who has less than 20% to use as a downpayment for a mortgage.

Let's take a look at a few options in the following example:

Sales Price Minus	10% downpayment Equals	Mortgage Balance
$250,000 -	$25,000 =	$225,000

THE GOOD: Option 1: 30 Year Fixed Mortgage

Interest Rate	Payment	Observations
5%	$1207	

If you choose option 1, the 30-year fixed mortgage, you have limited payment risk in the future. In the event rates decrease, you have the option of refinancing into a lower rate as long as you are making your mortgage payments on time.

THE BAD: Option 2: 5/1 Interest Only ARM

Interest Rate	Payment	Observations
5% (first 60 months)	$937	$270 monthly savings
7% (rate in month 61)	$1590	$653 increase in payment!!

If you choose option 2, the interest-only mortgage, you enjoy low payments for the first five years. But what happens at month 61 if your rate increases from 5% to 7%? First, the mortgage resets to 25 years (because 5 years have passed) and the rate increases to the maximum of 7%. You now will pay $1590 per month, an increase of 70%! What are the odds of your income increasing 70% per year? Do you see getting an 11% raise each year during the first five years of your mortgage to maintain the same mortgage debt-to-income ratio? In most cases, increasing payments without increasing income will cause an extreme hardship for any homeowner, especially in those instances when the homeowner has poor savings habits and the interest rate adjusts more frequently or more aggressively.

Understanding Mortgage Products – the Good, the Bad and the Ugly

THE UGLY: Option 3: Payment Option ARM

Interest Rate	Payment	Observations
1% minimum option	$723	$214 added to balance each month
5% interest only option	$937	
5% 30 year fixed option	$1207	
5% 15 year fixed option	$1779	
(the homeowner gets to choose a payment, each month, for the first five years)		
7% rate in month 61	$1681	balance is now $237,840!

If you choose option 3, the payment option ARM mortgage, then each month that you "pick" the minimum payment of $723, then $214 is ADDED to your mortgage balance because $937 is the minimum amount necessary to cover the interest due on your mortgage ($937 minus $723 equals $214 – and this is the amount added onto your mortgage balance each month). Because your mortgage balance is increasing instead of decreasing, this is called negative amortization. (With a regular mortgage, where you are required to pay towards your principal and interest, the balance decreases each month, and the loan is considered to be amortizing normally). What's more, because you are so tempted to make the minimum payment each month, when the mortgage resets at month 61, the new interest rate could very possibly be as high as 7%, the loan balance is now a whopping $237,840, and your monthly payment has increased by over $958! Add this ingredient to the mixture of decreasing property values and you potentially have a recipe for disaster.

Now, you may be asking yourself, *"who in his/her right mind would make the minimum payment each month?"* Well, unfortunately, millions of homebuyers got qualified for more expensive homes based upon the minimum payment as shown in the scenario above. In addition, because these homebuyers had more expensive homes that they really could not afford, they also had more expensive bills that went along with those homes (taxes, landscaping, furniture, and everything else that goes along with owning a "bigger" home). In many cases, these homeowners simply could not afford to make either of the higher payments even if they wanted to, so they got stuck making the lower payment, the mortgage balance began to increase instead of decrease, and then the nightmare began. Sad, but true.

THE PRESCRIPTION

While either of the products we described could prove to be beneficial to certain investors or buyers with different "symptoms," we want our readers to focus on getting a mortgage that they can afford and that enables them to live below their means and keep their home.

Therefore, we recommend a **30-year Fixed Rate Amortizing Mortgage** for most new homebuyers with a maximum housing debt ratio of 31% and a maximum total debt ratio of 41% (see Chapter 2, #8 for a quick lesson on debt ratio calculations).

A *dream home* is one that you can actually *dream in* . . . being able to sleep at night without worrying about your mortgage costs increasing is **priceless.**

PART TWO

Shopping for A Home: Find the House That's Right For You

Chapter Seven

**Selecting a Good Real Estate
Professional – Professional People
with a Purpose**

Chapter Seven

Selecting a Good Real Estate Professional –
Professional People with a Purpose

F inding a good real estate professional is a critical part of the homebuying process. There is no general rule of thumb regarding the years of experience that an agent has. An inexperienced agent could be an enthusiastic asset during your process, while an industry veteran may not be abreast of recent housing trends or new homebuying incentives – it's all based on the individual.

First, determine whether or not you want to work with an agent who also represents the seller. Remember, real estate agents are bound by laws that monitor their activities when representing either the buyer or seller, and when representing both the buyer and seller. In some instances, having an agent that represents you and the seller could be a good thing and in others, you may feel more comfortable having an agent that represents your interests exclusively. A good practice is to seek agent referrals from happy and successful homebuyers that you know, conduct an interview of each agent you consider working with, and listen to your gut. If something doesn't seem right, it probably isn't. If an agent is impatient or demonstrates an unnatural sense of urgency when asking you to sign certain documents, then you may want to take a step back and reconsider.

The following is a list of questions you may want to ask your agent or broker.

1. How many years of experience do you have in real estate and how many closings have you facilitated for buyers within the past twelve months? Can you provide proof?

2. Describe what good customer service means to you.

3. May I see a copy of your license?

4. What is your experience with first-time homebuyers / move-up buyers / investors / relocation buyers, etc.?

5. What is your experience with single family homes / duplexes / condominiums / townhomes / multi-unit buildings?

6. Can you provide me with the name and telephone number of three previous customers?

7. Do you have a list of referral partners for home inspections, legal concerns, appraisals, etc.?

8. Why should I choose you to assist me in the homebuying process?

9. Do you have any listings? If so, and I choose to purchase one of the listings in your inventory, will you represent both me and the seller?

10. Under what circumstances am I required to pay you a commission and do you require me to sign any type of buyer representation agreement?

Chapter Eight

Choosing a Home and Making An Offer – Time to Deal

Chapter Eight

Choosing a Home and Making An Offer – Time to Deal

C hoosing the home that is right for you and your family can be a tedious and time-consuming endeavor. In order to alleviate the stress, make sure you understand the process and try to avoid mistakes that will prevent you from achieving your dream.

Don't shop for homes above your preapproved price range. This is like going to the store for expensive champagne, knowing you only have beer money! It may be tempting to "just look and see," however this may set unrealistic expectations and compromise your reasoning. In addition, this is not a hobby for your real estate professional – it is hard work! Respect everyone's time by only seeing homes you can afford.

And one more thing – leave all of the extra tag-a-longs at home! Everyone has a different opinion and you may find yourself trying to please other people instead of pleasing yourself. They will be able to enjoy the home with you AFTER you close. The following is a step-by-step checklist to help you get through the home selection process.

1. **If you haven't done so already, <u>complete your loan application</u>**. Shopping for a home without a loan preapproval is like going to the mall with no money! You can't execute the transaction.

2. **Once you select the property you desire** and you wish to make an offer:

    a. Please confirm the property, taxes, and downpayment with your lender and make sure you can afford the payment – there are numerous cases where the buyer executes a contract only to find out later that the taxes or assessments result in a mortgage payment that is more than he/she can afford;

    b. At your Contract Consultation, your real estate agent should:

        i. Prepare your contract and answer all of your questions

        ii. Advise you of your rights and responsibilities

        iii. Ask for your signature on your offer so that your agent can present it to the seller or his/her representative.

    c. Wait for the seller's response. The seller has the option of accepting your offer, making a counter-offer, or rejecting your offer completely.

3. **After your offer is accepted**, the Attorney / Home Inspection Review Period begins:

    a. Your local agent must have your earnest money (certified funds) in his/her possession within 24 hours of acceptance by the seller;

    b. You typically have 5 business days (check the laws in

your state) to get a home inspection and to have your attorney review your contract and the details of your home inspection.

c. During this time, any changes to the contract should be submitted to the seller and/or the seller's representative. If there is no agreement of terms at this point, the buyer and/or seller has the right to cancel the contract and the buyer should be entitled to a refund of any earnest money submitted. This is known as a mutual separation agreement.

4. **After the Attorney / Home Inspection Review Period is complete:**

a. Your local agent will conduct your Contract Acceptance Consultation, where he/she will:

i. Review your accepted contract and answer any questions you may have;

ii. Provide you with a new What Happens Next Checklist & Moving Checklist; and

iii. Present you with everything you need to know as a homeowner about your new neighborhood;

b. Send a copy of your executed contract and earnest money deposit to your lender.

5. **After your loan is completely approved**:

    a   You should notify your attorney and the seller's attorney;

    b. You will be responsible for submitting final loan conditions to your lender and wait for your loan to get to "Clear to Close" status.

    c. You must pay for your Homeowners Insurance (one-year premium in advance) and provide proof to your lender;

    d. Your real estate professional will schedule your final walk through of the home and assist you with your moving checklist.

6. **After your final walk thru**:

    a. Notify your real estate professional and/or attorney in writing of any concerns you may have regarding the property and/or your loan;

    b. Verify you final closing figure with your lender.

7. **On the day of closing**:

    a. Don't forget your official state ID or driver's license;

    b. Verify the final amount you need to close with your attorney (your lender may be able to provide an estimate);

    c. Your funds must be in the form of a cashier's check made payable to you; and

d.   You, the seller, your attorney and the seller's attorney will meet at a title company or the attorney's office to close on your home. Your real estate professional will be present to answer any questions you may have, and your lender will be just a call away if any problems arise.

8.   **Move in and stay in!**

a.   Notify your real estate professional, home inspector, attorney, or lender of any immediate concerns, questions, or unexpected issues.

b.   Live below your means. Do not attempt to impress "friends" with a house full of new furniture that you cannot afford. The home is impressive enough!

PART THREE

Avoid Foreclosure: Keep Your House

Chapter Nine

Foreclosure Awareness and Prevention

Chapter Nine

Foreclosure Awareness and Prevention

Stuff Happens!

J ob loss, unforeseen medical conditions, and other life-altering occurrences can happen to anyone, causing you to fall behind in your loan payments. If you neglect paying your credit cards it hurts your credit rating; but if you stop paying your home loan, the situation is even worse, because the lender can foreclose and take ownership of the home.

Get Over Feeling Embarrassed

You must put your pride on hold if you're serious about stopping the foreclosure process and keeping your home.

Lenders do *not* want to foreclose, and will usually work with you to get you back on track. Your lender does not want to foreclose on your home because it is a very expensive proposition for a lender to do this and they hope to avoid it. Mortgage servicers do not want to own your home. Work with them!

In addition, no matter what anyone tells you and regardless of any scare tactics you have been exposed to, **YOU ARE STILL ON THE DEED TO YOUR HOME AND THEREFORE YOU HAVE RIGHTS AS A HOMEOWNER** – even during the foreclosure process – until a judicial foreclosure sale has taken place and in certain states, for a specific time period thereafter. No one can wake you up in the middle of the night and force you to leave your home, so don't be afraid to communicate. If the lender is able to determine, however, that you have abandoned the property, the lender will exercise its rights to protect its collateral by having the locks changed or otherwise securing the property.

Be Proactive: Call your Mortgage Servicer (the lender that is collecting your payments) immediately!

Your mortgage was given to you under very specific terms and secured by a mortgage, or Deed of Trust, on your home. Although it may seem cruel, these documents will dictate the actions of your mortgage servicer. If they don't follow the terms in these documents, to the letter, then investors will not invest in mortgage loans and that is bad for everyone.

Although lenders do not want to foreclose if it can be avoided, they do want to make sure you can follow through on any promises you make to bring your account current.

Tell it like it is!! Be prepared to share all details about your financial situation with your lender.

- An explanation of your current financial circumstances.

- Details about your current income.

- A list of your household expenses.

The lender will review and analyze your situation before offering a solution to bring your loan up-to-date.

Does the plan correct your situation?

Know your situation. How long is it going to take you to correct your financial situation? If your situation can be corrected in a few months, then this is clearly workable with your lender. On the other hand, if your situation is going to take more than three or four months to correct, you will need to seek more drastic action instead of hoping the lender will work with you. Lenders hands are tied by the contract you signed at your closing.

If your financial "bump in the road" is a three month situation then where can you dig up three months of mortgage payments? Family? 401(k) loan? IRA?

Consider borrowing money against a free and clear car. Some lenders will lend you $10,000 on just a signature. If you throw in the collateral of a car they may be more eager to help. Your possible damaged credit scores may prevent some types of help, but if you act soon enough, you can protect your credit score as well.

FACT: Most people get into trouble because they "hope" their financial storm will go away and simply end. Not happening! Instead, you must get objective help. Talk to the mortgage broker, real estate agent or loan officer who helped you get the loan in the first place and seek their help. If you don't have a trusting relationship with this person, seek a HUD Approved Counseling Agency by visiting www.HUD.gov.

Solutions for Temporary Problems

Reinstatement
Reinstatement might be possible when you are behind in your payments but can promise a lump sum to bring payments current

by a specific date.

Forbearance
In forbearance, you are allowed to delay payments for a short period, with the understanding that another option will be used at the end of the forbearance period to bring the account current. Lenders sometimes combine Forbearance with Reinstatement if you are able to demonstrate that you'll have the funds to bring your account current by a specific date.

A Repayment Plan
If your account is past due, but you can make payments going forward, the lender might agree to let you catch up by adding a portion of the past due amount to a certain number of monthly payments until your account is current.

Solutions for Longer-Term Problems

Mortgage Modification
If you can make your regular payment now, but cannot catch up on the past due amount, the lender might agree to modify your mortgage. One solution is to add the past due amount into your existing loan and finance it over a longer term.

Modification might also be possible if you no longer have the ability to make payments at the former level. The lender can modify your mortgage by extending the length of your loan, decreasing your mortgage balance, decreasing your interest rate, or a combination of the three.

Selling Your Home
If catching up is not a possibility, the lender might agree to put foreclosure on hold to give you some time to attempt to sell your home.

Deed in Lieu of Foreclosure

With this option, the lender allows you to give back your property and forgives the debt. It does have a negative impact on your credit record, but not as much as a foreclosure. The lender might require that you attempt to sell the house for a specific time period before agreeing to this option, and it might not be possible if there are other liens against the home.

For FHA Loans

The lender might be able to help you receive a one-time payment from the FHA Insurance fund. Your loan must be at least 4 months but no more than 12 months past due and you must show you are able to begin making full mortgage payments going forward.

- You must sign a promissory note, which allows HUD to place a lien on your property for the amount received from the fund.

- The note is interest free, but must eventually be repaid.

- The note becomes due when you pay off the loan or when you sell the property.

For VA Loans

The VA Regional Loan Centers offer financial counseling that's designed to help you avoid foreclosure. Call 1-800-827-1000 and ask for the phone number of the Loan Service Representative in your area.

Contact a HUD-Approved Counselor

If you don't want to talk with your lender alone, contact a HUD-approved counseling agency. A counselor can help you determine which options might be available to you and negotiate with your lender to work out a repayment program. You can find an approved agency at www.HUD.gov.

Get Your Credit Right

If your home loan is past due, your other obligations probably are too. A nonprofit credit counseling agency might be able to help you work with your creditors to reduce your monthly payments by lowering interest rates or extending repayment periods.

The key word here is *nonprofit*. Steer clear of companies that promise you quick, easy results for all of your credit problems in exchange for a large fee. You know better – that's not how it works in the real world. The National Foundation for Credit Counseling (www.nfcc.org) is a good place to start.

Get everything that you agree to with your lender in writing and then follow it to the letter!

Remember most people get into the "financial trouble" because they do not act soon enough. Move your ego aside and seek help early.

If you get behind on your mortgage payments, lenders are going to call. Answer their call and work with them.

Chapter Ten

Senior Citizens, Homeownership, and Financial Freedom

Chapter Ten

Senior Citizens, Homeownership, and Financial Freedom

What is a Reverse Mortgage?

A Reverse Mortgage or Reverse Home Mortgage is a financial product for seniors to use during retirement. When looking for ways to get cash from their home, most people consider selling their house or borrowing against their home equity and making monthly loan repayments on a home equity loan.

With a Reverse Home Mortgage, you get all the benefits of selling your house and all the benefits of getting a home equity loan - but you can still live in and retain ownership of your home and you don't have to pay back the loan. No matter how you structure a Reverse Mortgage, you typically don't pay anything back until you die, sell your home, or permanently move out. Furthermore, your ability to secure a Reverse Mortgage is not dependent on your credit history, income level, health or any other factors that might make a home equity loan expensive or problematic.

By converting your home equity into income, a Reverse Mortgage is a way to stay in your home and get cash to use for any purpose. There are no restrictions on how you can use money from a Reverse Mortgage.

So is a Reverse Mortgage for you and what's the catch?

Are you 62 years old and own your home?

Are you short on cash every month?

Do you wish you had money to repair your home, but you don't, and you can't borrow or make payments?

Are there rising medical costs you can't cover and your insurance doesn't cover them either?

Are you making a monthly payment that is keeping you from being able to live your life as you would like? Do you wish you could travel, or help a loved one, but you just don't have the funds in the bank to do so?

If you answered yes to any of the above, you might want to consider a Reverse Mortgage.

What are the pros and cons of reverse mortgages?

PROS OF REVERSE MORTGAGES

1. Allows you to stay in your home.

2. Pays off existing mortgages on the home.

3. Simple to qualify because credit score and income are not considered.

4. No monthly payments are due for as long as you live in the home.

5. You *receive* payments flexibly:

      a. Credit line for emergencies.

      b. Monthly income.

      c. Lump sum distribution.

      d. Any combination of the above.

6. A reverse mortgage can't get "upside down" so the heirs will never owe more than the home is worth.

7. Heirs inherit the home and keep all equity after the reverse mortgage is paid off.

8. Proceeds are not taxable.

9. The interest rate is lower than traditional mortgages and home equity loans.

CONS OF REVERSE MORTGAGES

1. The closing costs are about the same as the cost of selling your home. The largest cost is the FHA mortgage insurance and the other large cost is the origination fee (the lender's fee).

2. Although Social Security and Medicare are not affected, Medicaid and other need-based government assistance can be affected if you withdraw too much in one month.

3. The program is not well understood by most people and requires an independent HUD counseling session prior to receiving the reverse mortgage.

PART FOUR

**Understanding Credit and the Use of
Other People's Money**

Chapter Eleven

Credit Scoring and Your Future

Chapter Eleven

Credit Scoring and Your Future

What is Credit?

C redit is the use of someone else's money to pay for things and the promise to repay the money (loan) to the person or company who loaned it to you (the lender). Each of us has a credit history composed of our past experiences with credit. Credit reports document this history.

The Credit Laws

While laws do not guarantee that you will obtain credit, they do:

1.   Protect consumer rights and privacy

2.   Require businesses to give all consumers fair and equal opportunities

3.   Require businesses to ensure accurate information and resolve disputes over errors

The Equal Credit Opportunity Act (ECOA) prohibits the denial of credit because of sex, race, marital status, religion, national origin, age, or because you receive public assistance.

The Fair Credit Reporting Act grants consumer rights to learn information being distributed by credit reporting agencies.

What is a Credit Report and What Is Included in a Credit Report?

A credit report is a record of how you have paid your creditors and how much debt you have. Some of the items on your credit report are:

✓ Personal Identification Information (name, address, SSN, birth date, employment, etc.)

✓ Credit Account Information (date opened, credit limit, company, account number, activity, balance, etc.)

✓ Public Record Information (bankruptcy, liens, foreclosures, judgments, unpaid taxes, child support, monetary judgments, etc.)

✓ Collection Agency Account Information

✓ Additional Information (checking account closings, etc)

✓ Inquiries: A list of companies that requested your credit file that shows how often you have applied for credit in the past 24 months

✓ Pre-approved offers appear only on consumer reports

What's NOT on a Credit Report:

✓ Race

✓ Religion

✓ Medical history

- ✓ Personal Lifestyle

- ✓ Political preferences

- ✓ Criminal Record

- ✓ Gender

- ✓ Marital Status

- ✓ Nationality

What is a Credit Score?

- ✓ A numerical tool used to quickly access creditworthiness

- ✓ Snapshot of your credit risk at a particular point

- ✓ It is a number that helps lenders predict future credit performance of a borrower

- ✓ It changes as new information is added to your file

- ✓ Calculated by a computer

Credit Scores are Based on Five Main Categories:

- ✓ Payment history-35% of score

- ✓ Outstanding debt-30% of score

- ✓ Length of credit history-15% of score

- ✓ Inquiries-10% of score

✓   Types of credit-10% of score

How Do Creditors Determine Credit Value or Worthiness and Important Factors Affecting Credit Scoring:

✓   **Past payment performance and whether or not you've made payments on time**: 30- 60- and 90-day late payments will negatively impact your score. In addition, even if you are one day late, though it will not be reflected on your credit report, the lender may increase your interest rate or decrease your credit line, which could negatively impact your score.

✓   **Credit use: Are you over-extended or conservative?** If your account balances are near your credit limit, this will negatively impact your score. You should try to keep your balance less than 40% of your credit limit in order to improve and build your credit scores. Of course, this will not be possible at first for mortgage and auto debt, but you should maintain this as a practice for your credit cards and other revolving debt.

✓   **How long you have been using credit: the longer your credit history the better.** That's why it is NOT a good idea to close accounts that have a long positive payment history. Even if you pay off the debt, DO NOT close the account.

Credit Scores Range from 300 – 870 (average score 720)

While a "good score" depends on the scoring model and the lender, the following is a general scale in to help you determine where you fall on the credit score journey:

✓ 450-619 = Poor (Sinking, a life jacket is available)

✓ 620-659 = Fair (Rough Waves)

✓ 660-749 = Good (Smooth Sailing)

✓ 750 and Higher = Excellent (Cruising on Automatic)

Remember: The Higher Your Score The Lower Your Interest Rate (in most cases)!

PART FIVE

Questions About Buying a Home

Chapter Twelve

Frequently Asked Questions: General Homeowership

Chapter Twelve

Frequently Asked Questions: General Homeowership

Q : With all that is going on in the economy, is now a good time to purchase real estate?

A: Yes, now is a great time to purchase real estate, and home ownership is the foundation for building wealth. Until you own where you live, many other investment vehicles remain out of reach for most Americans. With homes in many areas at affordable prices, now is a great time to buy at record low prices, hold on to your investment, and receive the tax and other benefits afforded to homeowners. The home you couldn't afford last year or two years ago may be in an affordable price range for you today.

Q: What are the steps to buying a home?

A: After you make the decision to build wealth through real estate and become a homeowner, you should do the following:

1. **Get educated**. Taking a home ownership education course will provide you with the general knowledge necessary to get a home, select knowledgeable professionals, and keep your home (avoid and prevent foreclosure). You may search for a HUD approved non-profit housing counselor at. http://www.hud.gov/offices/hsg/sfh/hcc/hcc_home.cfm.

2. **Get preapproved.** Contact a mortgage professional to determine your approval amount. Suggestion: instead of asking, *"How much can I buy?"* you should ask *"This is how much I can afford to pay monthly for housing, so how much of a home will my pre-determined budget allow me to purchase?"* Most real estate agents and down payment programs require a preapproval prior to working with you.

3. **Get a real estate agent.** Work with a local real estate professional who will listen to your desires and help you shop for a home that falls within your price range. Some real estate agents may require that you sign a buyer-representation agreement for a mutually agreeable time period. In the event your agent requires you to sign a buyer representation, suggest 30-day increments or less to ensure that the buyer/agent relationship is one that meets your needs. In most cases, a real estate agent should not charge you a fee for buyer representation (if you are selling a home however, seller paid commissions are usual and customary).

4. **Make your offer.** You can offer whatever you like, but keep in mind that the seller has expenses and obligations (mortgage debt to pay off, attorney's fees, etc.) as well, so try to make your highest and best offer during the negotiating process. Be sure to ask for any closing cost assistance, known repair requests, and other items you desire at this time. It will be too late to negotiate after your offer is accepted.

5. **Submit your earnest money.** If your offer is accepted, you will be required to submit earnest money, preferably in certified funds, to your agent or to the seller's agent. Earnest money is usually $1,000 or one percent of the sales price for

average priced existing homes, but is often higher for luxury homes and/or new construction homes. This money is applied to your down payment at the time of closing and is only refundable when certain conditions are met (your loan is denied; there are irreconcilable issues during the attorney review period – please check with your local real estate attorney and the laws in your state).

6. **Attorney review & home inspection**. Check with your local real estate attorney, but in most states, there is a five-day attorney review period. You should obtain a home inspection, which will normally take anywhere from 1 ½ hours to 2 hours and will include a detailed overview of the condition of the home and its major systems. During this time, any issues relating to the home inspection, contract terms, and other matters must be addressed; otherwise, the buyer may forfeit certain rights. Please get a real estate attorney. You would not go to a foot doctor for brain surgery, so please be careful when choosing the appropriate attorney to represent you in one of the largest investments you will every make.

7. **Mortgage Commitment**. Your lender will need the contract, proof and source of earnest money, and updated pay stubs, bank statements, and other financial information. You will receive a Good Faith Estimate and a Truth in Lending disclosure, which will outline the terms of your loan, interest rate, annual percentage rate, closing costs, and down payment. An appraisal will be ordered to determine the fair market value and general condition of the home (this is separate and distinct from a home inspection). If you are putting down less than 20 percent and the loan requires mortgage insurance, your lender will obtain mortgage

insurance at this time. This is not to be confused with homeowners/hazard insurance. You will need to contact your local insurance agent to obtain hazard insurance to protect your home against certain perils like fire, theft, and damage. Finally, after the lender has reviewed all of the above, a Loan Commitment will be issued that will list any additional items required by the buyer or seller prior to closing.

8.   **Final Walk Through**. Your agent should arrange a final walk-through of the home prior to closing (if you are purchasing new construction, you may need to do several walk-throughs at different phases in the building process). Ensure that any written commitments relating to repairs have been met and address any outstanding issues with your agent and/or real estate attorney.

9.   **Confirm Your Cash to Close**. Confirm the final amount you will need to bring to the closing with your lender and/or real estate attorney. Depending on whether or not the closing agent has received final details from both the buyer and the seller, this may or may not be available. If not, don't panic! Refer to your Good Faith Estimate provided by your lender and bring the amount you need in the form of a cashier's check along with your official ID. Any excess funds will be refunded to you immediately at the closing.

10. **Move in and stay in**. Move in your new home and don't try to "keep up with the Joneses'"! Maintain your budget and live within your means. Utilize bonuses, tax refunds, and other additional cash flow to improve your property and increase your six-month savings and emergency fund. Save separately for new furniture and pay for it with cash if and

only if you have the rest of your financial house in order! If you are going to miss a mortgage payment, reach out to your lender or a HUD-approved counselor right away to discuss options.

Q: I currently own a home and I am not sure if I want to sell it or rent it out when I buy my new home. What advice do you have?

A: In order to qualify for your new home, you will need to either sell your current property, or rent it out. If you choose to rent the property, you should have six months of mortgage payments saved for each property you own or plan to own and even more importantly, you should have a positive cash flow. For example, if the mortgage, taxes, insurance and assessments on your current home are $600 and you can rent the property out for $1000 or more, then you will have $400 in positive monthly cashflow. You can invest the $400 into other wealth creation streams to ensure a comfortable retirement and/or education planning for your children. If you have less than $400 per month in positive cash flow, then selling the property might be a better option, because unexpected repairs or unstable tenants can jeopardize your cashflow and your credit if you are unable to keep up with the payments.

Actual Monthly Cashflow Calculation for Rental Property

$1,000	-	$600	=	$400 actual monthly cashflow
Actual		(piti*)		
Rental income				

*piti = principal, interest, taxes and insurance

Caution: even though you may have $1000 in rental income, for example, the lender will deduct 25% or more of the rental income when determining your eligibility for the loan. The 25% is called a "vacancy factor," which essentially means there is a 25% chance that the property will be vacant at some time in the future.

Qualifying Cashflow Calculation for Rental Property

$1,000	x	25%	=	$250
Actual		vacancy		underwriting
Rental income		factor		deduction

$1,000	-	$250	=	$750
Actual		underwriting		Qualifying
Rental income		deduction		Rental Income

$750	-	$600	=	$150
Qualifying		(piti*)		Qualifying
Rental income				Cashflow

Deciding whether or not to sell your property can be tricky, and it depends on your long term investment objectives. If the property is in a high appreciation market, where property values are steadily increasing, you may want to consider holding the property and cashing out at some time in the future when you can reap the benefit of this investment. If, on the other hand, you have already experienced rapid appreciation and the market is slowing down, or even worse, you have held the property for several years and it has not experienced any significant growth in value, then now may be the time to cut your losses, sell the property, and move on to a better opportunity.

In short, there is no easy answer. But one piece of advice is certain: Don't Fall In Love With the Walls! Successful real estate investing requires more business logic and less emotion. Each piece of property you acquire should be a part of an overall plan to help you achieve wealth in the future.

Q: I want to buy new construction. What are some of the things I should consider that are not in the normal

homebuying process?

A: Building a home, townhome, condo, or multi-unit property requires a significant amount of patience and planning. Here are a few things to consider:

1. Earnest Money Deposit: while the earnest money deposit for existing properties range anywhere from $1,000 to $5,000, depending on the price, location, and market standards, the average earnest money deposit for new construction ranges anywhere from three to ten percent of the purchase price. Because the builder is taking a risk by building your property, he wants to be assured that you will not walk away from the deal and therefore will require a higher earnest money deposit before beginning any building activities. You may consider asking for a payment plan, perhaps $2500 down and $1000 to $2500 monthly until your entire earnest money deposit has been tendered.

2. Home Inspection: you should request a 5 phase home inspection from an independent inspector that you hire to inspect the property (1) when the foundation is complete; (2) when the frame is complete; (3) when the mechanical, electrical and plumbing systems are in and **before** the drywall is installed; (4) after the drywall has been installed and **before** the painting; and 5) final walkthrough prior to closing. This will be more expensive than the traditional home inspection, but it is worth it to secure your peace of mind when building your new home.

3. Selections and Upgrades: Check to see what is included

and what is not included in the asking prices. Everything that is not included is considered an upgrade. Here are a few basic items that you want to consider:

a. Light fixtures that you see in the model typically are not included in the price;

b. Extra electrical outlets or placement of electrical outlets;

c. Extra cable connections;

d. Extra telephone wiring (ask for multiline wiring to accommodate your phone, fax, internet);

e. Garbage disposal; and/or

f. Water filter line for the refrigerator.

4. Delayed Closing – Unexpected Issues: because your closing will be 4 to 6 months in the future, a change in your credit or employment, changes in the market prices, and changes in interest rates may affect your ability to purchase.

5. Home Warranty: ask the builder for a two-year home warranty, guaranteed by a third party. You want to make sure it is a third party because if the builder guarantees the home and a major issue occurs, the builder may not have the financial resources to resolve your issues depending on the cost of repairs.

6. Empty Shell: your new home will, in most cases, be an

empty shell. You will need to purchase grass, trees, window screens and shades, light bulbs, and many other things that are automatically included in an existing home. Be sure to consider these costs in your budget.

Chapter Thirteen

Frequently Asked Questions: Credit

Chapter Thirteen

Frequently Asked Questions: Credit

With Contributions by Harrine Freeman
(www.hefreemanenterprises.com)

Q : **How do I establish credit to purchase a home if I don't have any credit cards or loans?**

A: You can use a service called "Pay Rent Build Credit", www.prbc.com that uses non-traditional forms of credit such as: cell phones, utilities, child support, and alimony to establish a credit report separate from Equifax, Experian and TransUnion and can be used to help get approved for a mortgage loan. You can also get a secured credit card and request the account be reported to the 3 major credit bureaus, Equifax, Experian and TransUnion.

Q: If I file for bankruptcy can I still be approved for a mortgage loan?

A: Yes, but you may receive a higher interest rate and may not get the best deal. Although you can receive an FHA market interest rate mortgage while you are still paying off a Chapter 13 bankruptcy (as long as you have been paying on time for at least one year and have no other negative credit since the bankruptcy) and one year after the discharge of a Chapter 7 bankruptcy (if the bankruptcy was filed due to an uncontrollable circumstance like death, divorce, or medical illness), most programs require that you wait two years before applying for a mortgage loan and many require that you wait for four years. Following our Mortgage Approval Plan will assist you along your path to homeownership. It's important to remember to pay all of your bills on time after a bankruptcy if you wish to get approved for a mortgage in the future.

Q: How do I fix errors on my credit report and get approved for a mortgage?

A: Get a recent copy of your credit report within the past 3 months. Review everything and write down everything that is not correct. Send a dispute letter to each credit bureau reporting the error and provide any documentation you have to support your claim of incorrect information being reported. You can also dispute the information online at each credit bureau's website. Disputing information online takes two weeks to receive a response, while disputing information by mail takes 30 days to receive a response. You may also get copies of these forms and important steps in the Mortgage Approval Plan.

During the mortgage application process, you may also request that your loan officer obtain a Residential Mortgage Credit Report (RMCR) to submit to the underwriter with your mortgage application. The RMCR will provide a quick update of the incorrect information and allow the underwriter to see what your credit report would look like in its improved state. The RMCR is also a quick way to have non-traditional credit lines (like rent, utility payments, cell phone payments, child support payments, etc.) added to your credit report in the event you have little or no credit. You may also request a "re-score" (resulting in a higher credit score and possibly a better loan and interest rate) along with the RMCR for a fee.

Q: How long does negative information stay on my credit report?

A: Most negative information (late payments or unpaid bills) can appear on your credit report for 7 years. Bankruptcies can remain for 7 to 10 years. Bounced checks remain for 2 years. Unpaid judgments (court order to pay a bill) can remain for up to 20 years. Unpaid tax liens (when taxes are owed on a house, car or other asset) can remain for up to 7 years or more.

Q: What should I do if I am applying for a mortgage but my credit has been negatively impacted as a result of identity theft?

A: If someone steals your identity and opens an account in your name without your knowledge, you should:

1. Contact the company, close the affected account and open a new one. If the account required a PIN, create a new one.

2. Contact the credit bureaus and ask to speak to someone in the Fraud Department. Request a 90-day security alert, which alerts creditors to confirm the consumer's identity before extending credit.

3. Request that your name be removed from pre-screened credit offer lists.

4. Request a copy of your credit report.

5. File a police report.

6. Contact the companies you do business with and inform

them you have been a victim of identity theft.

7. Contact your local post office and inform them you have been a victim of identity theft.

8. Contact your local Social Security Administration and inform them you have been a victim of identity theft.

9. Save all written documentation above to submit with your mortgage application. You will need extensive evidence to obtain a mortgage approval if identity theft has negatively impacted your credit report.

Q: A collection agency contacted me about a 10-year-old debt. Do I still have to pay it?

A: Check to see if the statute of limitations (time period a company has available to pursue collecting a debt) has expired. If it has expired, you are not legally obligated to pay the debt and it should be removed from your credit report. If it has not expired, then the company is still able to pursue, and accordingly, you should contact the company to set up a payment plan. http://www.creditinfocenter.com/rebuild/statuteLimitations.sht ml#2.

Chapter Fourteen

Frequently Asked Questions: Mortgage

Chapter Fourteen

Frequently Asked Questions: Mortgage

Q : **I am putting down less than 20 percent and my loan requires private mortgage insurance. Will I have to pay this forever?**

A: No. When you have more than 20% equity in your home, mortgage insurance is no longer required. Let's look at this example. If your home is valued at $100,000 at the time of purchase, then you are eligible to have your mortgage insurance removed when the balance is less than $80,000. Conversely, if your home increases in value, and your balance is less than 80% of the new value, then you should contact your lender and request an appraisal from a licensed appraiser that is approved by your lender in order to substantiate your new value.

It is important to note that even if your loan does not require mortgage insurance, the cost of your being a higher risk has been met, in most cases, by charging you a higher interest rate. Please visit www.smartermi.com to get more information about mortgage insurance and tax deductibility, free job loss insurance, homebuyer privileges discounts, how to receive up to a $500 gift card after closing (not available in all states), and more!

Q: I am a first time homebuyer. What down payment assistance programs are available?

A: There are hundreds, possibly thousands, of programs available to first time homebuyers. Many vary by state, and some are even available to those who are not purchasing real estate for the first time, as long as the buyer intends to live in the property. Trying to find a program without an adequate analysis from a seasoned mortgage professional is like calling the doctor with a cough and wanting to know if you have a cold or cancer! The doctor must take your blood work if you want a proper diagnosis. Likewise, your lender will need to obtain extensive details about you in order to properly diagnose you with the down payment assistance program and mortgage that is best for you.

Q. The property I have chosen needs repairs, but I am a first-time homebuyer with limited cash. Is there help for me?

A: Yes, the Federal Housing Administration (FHA) 203(k) Rehabilitation loan may be the answer to your prayers. With this loan, you can roll the cost of minor repairs (up to $35,000) into the Streamline (K) loan.

If your repairs exceed $35,000, or if you need major repairs and renovations, then you can roll the total rehabilitation costs into the regular 203(k) loan up to the loan limit in your county or your approved loan amount, whichever is less.

In addition, you can convert a 4 unit building into a 2 unit or vice versa, and you can use this program to acquire mixed use property (residential area combined with commercial space such as a beauty shop, day care facility, etc) and maximize your cash flow. For example, you may wish to have a hair salon on the first floor and three apartments upstairs; this is acceptable with the 203(k) loan as long as the total number of units is 4 or less and you can obtain this mortgage with only 3.5% as a downpayment! For more information on the FHA 203(k) Rehabilitation Loan, visit http://www.hud.gov/offices/hsg/sfh/203k/203kmenu.cfm.

Q: I am a veteran. What options are available for me?

A: The VA loan program is an excellent option because it requires no down payment, has no mortgage insurance, and like the FHA loan, requires no minimum credit score (though there are credit guidelines that must be adhered to). Moreover, the VA loan can be used to acquire 1 – 4 unit properties and the spouse of an active duty veteran can purchase real estate while the active duty veteran is overseas.

Q: What should I know about adjustable rate mortgages?

A: Adjustable rate mortgages are not necessarily bad, depending on your situation. In some cases, adjustable rate mortgages can help keep your mortgage payments low during the first few years of the mortgage. However, there are a few things to consider if you do in fact accept an adjustable rate mortgage.

1. **fixed period:** usually 1, 2, 3, or 5 years, this is the period of time your interest rate will remain fixed before it adjusts. If the fixed period is less than one year, beware. If the fixed period is 5 years, for example, and you only plan to live in the home for less than 5 years, then a 5 year adjustable rate mortgage may be a good option.

2. **market index:** this is what will be used to determine your interest rate in the future. For example, the FHA adjustable rate mortgage is based on the one-year treasury bill index. Other mortgages may be tied to higher, more volatile indexes, so please beware!

3. **margin:** the margin will be added to the index to determine your new interest rate when it is time for your interest rate to adjust. *The lender may have an option to choose which margin you can get, so make sure you ask! Often, lenders will automatically give you the higher margin because the loans with higher margins pay higher commissions.* So if the one-year treasury bill index is 2.5% and the margin on your loan is 2%, then your new rate will be 2.5% plus 2%, which is 4.5% (your adjustment cap must also be considered, as indicated in number 4 below).

4. **adjustment cap:** this is the maximum amount that your interest rate can change, up or down, during any adjustment period. So let's use the example in three above.

Current Rate	index	+ margin	=	adj rate	adj cap	actual new rate
4.0	2.5	2.0		4.5	1.0	4.5
4.0	3.5	2.0		5.5	1.0	5.0*
4.0	0.5	2.0		2.5	1.0	3.0**

*even though the adjusted rate would be 5.5 when you add the index and the margin, the adjustment cap limits the change to a maximum of one percent. Since the current rate is 4.0, the new rate cannot go higher than 5.0.

**even though the adjusted rate would be 2.5 when you add the Index and the margin, the adjustment cap limits the change to a maximum of one percent. Since the current rate is 4.0, the new rate cannot be lower than 3.0.

5. **life cap:** this is the maximum amount that your interest rate can change, up or down, over the life of the loan.

Chapter Fifteen

Frequently Asked Questions: Legal Issues

Chapter Fifteen

Frequently Asked Questions: Legal Issues

With Contributions by Attorney Deadra Woods Stokes
(www.yourwealthcounselor.com)

Q : **Should I purchase real estate with my significant other (or brother / sister / friend / cousin, etc.)?**

A: "You should be careful when mixing business with pleasure!" Purchasing real estate is just that: a business transaction. Despite popular belief, marriage actually affords individuals a legal benefit to share in the assets acquired during the course of the marriage. In some states, it also includes those items acquired prior to the marriage and brought into the marriage and maintained by both parties during the course of the marriage in some form or fashion. Therefore if you "must" purchase real estate with a joint owner who is not your spouse, then you "must"follow these rules:

1. Ensure that both of your names appear on the title of the property at some point only after the following nine (9) points have been completed as written below. If you fail to complete 2-10, you cannot do #1.

2. Determine the legal manner in which title will be taken (i.e., joint tenancy or tenants-in-common) if both of your names will appear on title. For example, if upon your death you

want your share of the property to pass to your children or your heirs instead of to the joint owner of the property, you would hold the property as"tenants-in-common". If you want your share to go "only" to the joint owner, then "joint tenancy" would be your best choice. (Check with your local real estate attorney regarding your state's applicable laws)

3. Talk to a real estate attorney (not a criminal / civil / accident / etc. attorney)to sort out the options available in your state and decide what should occur with each of your respective shares if you were to become disabled, terminally ill, or pass away.

4. Find out if either party is currently married or is currently going through a divorce. (You might find yourself in a legal battle with your joint owner's spouse whom he/she failed to discuss with you.)

5. Make sure you are aware of all of the children of your joint owner/significant other (the real estate might become subject to litigation in a child support proceeding).

6. Have your joint owner provide a current copy of his/her credit report. (Note: all judgments and tax liens will attach to the real estate when real property is transferred via a Quit Claim Deed. Therefore if your joint owner has a judgment for an outstanding child support matter or any other matter, that lien will automatically attach to the real estate that you now own together).

7. Develop a plan for the real estate in case either of you elect not to remain in the relationship/partnership/friendship.

8. Have a minimum of six (6) months of full mortgage

payments saved (not just your share) in case of an emergency/break-up/argument or other unfortunate event.

9. Determine the roles that you will have with respect to the real estate. Who will maintain the property?, Who will pay the bills associated with the property?

10. Write out your answers to questions 2-9 and then answer question #1. **AFTER all answers to questions 1-10 are in writing, then you may consider purchasing property with a friend/family member/significant other that you are not legally married to.**

Q: If the Seller verbally promises in front of others to complete certain repairs and later decides at closing not to make the repairs, is the Seller liable? Can I make him complete the repairs as promised since I have witnesses?

A: If the promise is not in writing and it relates to real estate, it is typically not enforceable. Therefore you must check with an attorney in your area, but in most instances you will not be able to enforce the verbal promise.

Q: If I am separated from my spouse and I decide to purchase real estate, is my spouse still entitled to my real estate even though he/she did not contribute to the purchase of the real property?

A: If you are not legally separated (by way of an order entered by the court) and are simply living separate and apart, you are still considered to be legally married despite where the two of you choose to live. Therefore, in most jurisdictions the property is still deemed "marital property" even if your spouse's name is not on the property and your spouse, in most instances, is entitled to his/her respective interest as determined by the laws of the state where you both reside.

Q: Now that I am a homeowner, do I need an estate plan, a trust, or both?

A: Yes, and yes!! First you want to put your property in a land trust. This will provide you with a certain amount of privacy in ownership and will facilitate the transfer of your property in the event of your death. This is not the same as a will (which you also need). If you leave your home to someone via a will, the will can be contested and stay in probate court for years, preventing your intended heir from enjoying the property. On the other hand, if your property is held in a land trust, then upon your death, ownership transfers easily to whomever is designated as the beneficiary in your trust, similar to an insurance policy.

You also need an estate plan. This will allow you to create generational wealth. This is like a business plan after your death. You get to determine who gets what, and when they get it. For example, you may choose to designate funds from your life insurance policy to pay off you mortgage, then the remaining funds can be allocated to your children, spouse, or loved one on a monthly or annual basis for their care. This is an important step in the homeownership process that is often overlooked.

Chapter Sixteen

Frequently Asked Questions: Insurance

Chapter Sixteen

Frequently Asked Questions: Insurance

With Contributions by Curtis R. Monday
(www.curtismonday.net)

 : How much does homeowner's insurance cost?

A: The price of a homeowner's insurance policy is determined by several factors. The age of the property, size of the property, inside amenities, location and type of construction are examples of the different factors that can affect the price. Unless there are extreme market conditions (like Hurricane Katrina New Orleans flooding), a homebuyer should budget $600 to $1500 for the annual cost of a homeowner's insurance policy.

Q: What is replacement cost coverage?

A: Replacement cost coverage seeks to restore a homeowner back to his/her original state when a loss is experienced. Replacement cost coverage seeks to give you what it would cost in today's dollars to replace any property (furniture, jewelry, clothing, etc.) that was lost or damaged. Replacement cost coverage in a homeowner's policy is the superior coverage because it protects the homeowner from receiving a depreciated or actual cash value settlement in the event of a claim.

Q: Does my homeowner's policy protect me against floods?

A: The homeowner's insurance policy will protect you against "named perils." Fire, lightning, theft, vandalism and wind are some of the more common instances that are covered under the policy. Flood protection is NOT covered under the basic homeowner's insurance policy. A flood policy is a separate federally sponsored insurance policy. If the area where your home is located is within a flood zone (or an area that historically is plagued by flooding) AND if there is a mortgage on the property, the mortgage company will require you to purchase a separate flood insurance policy.

Q: What is mortgage insurance and do I need it?

For many homebuyers, mortgage insurance may not be the most celebrated form of insurance, but, for some, it's an absolute must. For those individuals who wouldn't typically be able to afford a large 20 percent down payment, it's a "foot in the door," allowing for homeownership with as little as a 3 to 5 percent down payment.

A: There are two primary types of mortgage insurance (MI) they are FHA and Private Mortgage Insurance (PMI). Mortgage Insurance is an affordable, predictable and cancelable way to buy a home with a low down payment. The premiums paid may even be tax deductible. It allows qualified borrowers to finance a home with a down-payment as little as three-and-a-half percent.

Mortgage Insurance protects your lender against non-payment should you default on your loan. It's important to understand that mortgage insurance protects your lender—not you. As the buyer of this coverage, you're paying the premiums, so that your lender is protected. MI is often required by lenders due to the higher level of default risk that's associated with low down payment loans. In the industry it's been proven that the more borrowers invests in the home they are purchasing, the less likely they are to default and walk away from the home. Consequently, the mortgage insurance benefit to you is a lower down payment mortgage and the ability to become a homeowner sooner.

Q: How much does Mortgage Insurance cost?

A: The average costs of mortgage insurance premiums vary, but they typically fall between one-half and one percent of the loan amount, depending on the size of the down payment and loan specifics. On a $200,000 loan with a $10,000 down payment, you might expect to pay somewhere around $85 a month, or about $1000 a year, in addition to your mortgage payment.

Q: What is the difference between Private Mortgage Insurance and Mortgage Protection Insurance?

A: Private mortgage insurance and mortgage protection insurance are often confused. Though they sound similar, they're two totally different types of insurance products.

Mortgage protection insurance (also known as mortgage life insurance) is essentially a life insurance policy designed to pay off your mortgage in the event of your death.

Private mortgage insurance (PMI), is an affordable, predictable, cancelable and tax deductible* way to buy a home with a low down payment. It allows qualified borrowers to finance a home with a down-payment of less than twenty percent. PMI, like FHA, protects the lender if the borrower defaults (fails to pay) on the mortgage loan. These two products should never be construed as substitutes for each other.

* Consult an accountant to determine if you're eligible for a mortgage insurance tax deduction.

Q: How can I cancel or terminate my PMI?

A: So, you don't like the idea of making those extra mortgage insurance payments? Once your Loan-to-Value (LTV) ratio is 80% or less, you may be able to cancel your PMI. Your LTV ratio is the mortgage balance owed divided by the current market value of the home.

LTV = 1st Mortgage Balance Owed ÷ Current Market Value

Here are a few ways to eliminate mortgage insurance altogether:

1. APPRAISAL
    If the value of your home has increased in recent years, you may be able to cancel your mortgage insurance. Once the balance on your mortgage falls below 80 percent of the current market value of your home, in most cases you can cancel your private mortgage insurance. You would, of course, need to present your lender with a valid home appraisal before cancellation can occur. The costs associated with getting an appraisal may or may not be worthwhile, depending on your unique mortgage situation.

2. REMODEL
    It's the same principle as above. By making home improvements, you may increase the market value of your house, getting you that much closer to the all-important 80 percent "LTV" level.

3. PAY DOWN YOUR MORTGAGE
    Paying down your mortgage may also be a viable option.

Making even small additional payments each month can make a big difference over time. Once you get that loan-to-value-ratio below 80 percent, in most cases you'll no longer be required to make PMI payments.

4. AUTOMATIC TERMINATION
    Thanks to The Homeowner's Protection Act (HPA) of 1998, you have the right to request private mortgage insurance cancellation when your LTV ratio is 80% or less. What's more, lenders are required to automatically cancel PMI coverage when a 78 percent loan-to-value is reached. Some exceptions to these provisions, such as liens on property or not keeping up with payments, may require further PMI coverage.

Without a doubt, private mortgage insurance has proven invaluable for families trying to attain the American Dream of homeownership. It affords these individuals an opportunity that isn't always easily achieved in an often inflated real estate market. Paying more or longer than needed isn't prudent, and it's highly recommended that all steps be taken to avoid unnecessary payment of PMI. Knowing when to cancel can save you thousands, so be sure to utilize all the resources available to you and cancel when you reach the proper LTV ratio.

Legislation has passed making PMI insurance tax deductible, much like mortgage interest and property taxes. There are some restrictions, such as the property must be your primary residence, your adjusted gross income must be $100k or less for full deduction (partial deductions up to $109K), and the origination of your mortgage must have occurred on or after January 1, 2007. Lawmakers have *extended this private mortgage insurance tax deduction through 2010.* **Please consult a tax advisor regarding your specific situation.**

Q: What is mortgage life or credit life insurance?

A: This is the same as mortgage protection insurance. Mortgage protection insurance is essentially a life insurance policy designed to pay off your mortgage in the event of your death.

PART SIX

Home Ownership Resources

Associations and Organizations

1. **National Associations and Organizations**
   a. American Society of Appraisers: www.appraisers.org

   b. American Society of Home Inspectors: www.ashi.org

   c. Asian Real Estate Association of America: www.areaa.org

   d. Mortgage Bankers Association: www.mbaa.org

   e. National Association of Consumer Bankruptcy Attorneys: www.nacba.org

   f. National Association of Hispanic Real Estate Professionals: www.nahrep.org

   g. National Association of Mortgage Brokers: www.namb.org

   h. National Association of Real Estate Brokers: www.nareb.com

   i. National Association of Realtors: www.realtor.com

2. **Department of Housing and Urban Development Resources and Programs**: www.hud.gov
   a. Federal Housing Administration (FHA) Loan

   b. Teacher Next Door Program

   c. Reverse Equity Conversion Mortgage Program

3. **Free Real Estate Legal Advice:**
www.real-estate-law.freeadvice.com

4. **Government Organizations and Government Sponsored Entities (GSEs):**
   a. **Ginnie Mae**: www.ginniemae.gov

   b. **Fannie Mae**: www.fanniemae.com

   c. **Freddie Mac**: www.freddiemac.com

5. **HUD Approved Housing Counselors:**
www.hud.gov/offices/hsg/sfh/hcc/hcc_home.cfm

6. **Laws and Legislation**
   a. **Equal Credit Opportunity Act / Federal Trade Commission**: www.ftc.gov (see consumer protection)

   b. **Fair Housing Act**:
www.hud.gov./offices/fheo/FHLaws/index.cfm

   c. **Real Estate Settlement Procedures Act (RESPA)**:
www.hud.gov/offices/hsg/ramh/res/respa_hm.cfm

7. **Private Mortgage Insurance**: www.privatemi.com

8. **Veteran's Administration**: www.homeloans.va.gov

Forms You Can Use

DOCUMENTS NEEDED FOR MORTGAGE APPROVAL

❏ 1040 TAX RETURNS AND W2 FORMS: if there are any gaps in employment please write a letter of explanation and explain – make the timeline very clear to the underwriter – you may want to set this up like a resume, just remember, there should be no gaps!

❏ YEAR-TO-DATE PROFIT AND LOSS STATEMENT IF YOU ARE SELF EMPLOYED

❏ LAST 2 PAY STUBS or LAST 4 IF YOU GET PAID EVERY WEEK

❏ LAST 2 MONTHS BANK STATEMENTS and OTHER ASSETS

❏ RECENT COLLEGE OR TRADE SCHOOL GRADUATES: (1) COPY OF CERTIFICATE / DEGREE; (2) LETTER OF EMPLOYMENT IN YOUR FIELD OF STUDY; (3) 1ST PAYSTUB

❏ LEGIBLE COPY OF DRIVER'S LICENSE (or other state approved identification) AND LEGIBLE COPY OF SOCIAL SECURITY CARD

❏ $_____ APPLICATION FEE

❏ NAME, ADDRESS, AND PHONE # OF LANDLORD

- ❏ LAST 12 MONTHS CANCELLED CHECKS FOR RENT/MORTGAGE OR A LETTER FROM YOUR LANDLORD INDICATING THE DATE YOU BEGAN RENTING AND THAT YOU PAY ON TIME EVERY MONTH

- ❏ COURT ORDER IF YOUR RECEIVE CHILD SUPPORT INCOME / ALIMONY **OR** A SIGNED AGREEMENT FOR CHILD SUPPORT / ALIMONY **PLUS** PROOF THAT THE CHILD SUPPORT / ALIMONY PAYMENTS HAVE BEEN RECEIVED FOR THE LAST 12 MONTHS **AND / OR** A COPY OF THE DIVORCE DECREE

- ❏ PROOF STUDENT LOANS ARE DEFERRED AT LEAST ONE YEAR FROM CLOSING DATE

- ❏ LEASE IN THE AMOUNT OF _____ FOR CURRENT PROPERTY OR

- ❏ PROOF OF SALE OF CURRENT PROPERTY PRIOR TO CLOSING ON NEW HOME

- ❏ COMPLETE COPIES OF BANKRUPTCY DISCHARGE PAPERS, INCLUDE ALL SCHEDULES

- ❏ CHAPTER 13 PAYMENT HISTORY

- ❏ PERMISSION FROM CHAPTER 13 TRUSTEE TO ENTER MORTGAGE TRANSACTION

- ❏ GIFT LETTER, IF APPLICABLE, OR OTHER EVIDENCE OF FUNDS TO CLOSE

❏ SOCIAL SECURITY AWARDS LETTER + PROOF RECEIVED LAST TWO MONTHS

❏ IF SOCIAL SECURITY IS FOR A CHILD, PLEASE SEND A COPY OF THE CHILD'S BIRTH CERTIFICATE (IF CHILD IS 15 OR OVER, YOU NEED PROOF IT WILL CONTINUE PAST AGE 18)

❏ IF SOCIAL SECURITY IS FOR A DISABILITY, PLEASE SEND PROOF THAT DISABILITY IS EXPECTED TO CONTINUE AT LEAST 3 YEARS

❏ EVIDENCE OF MONTHLY PENSION RECEIVED (LETTER AND PAYSTUB)

❏ CREDIT REFERENCE LETTERS IF YOU HAVE LITTLE OR NO CREDIT

❏ LETTER OF EXPLANATION (LOX or LOE) FOR DEROGATORY CREDIT

❏ PROOF THAT COLLECTIONS / JUDGMENTS HAVE BEEN PAID IN FULL

❏ COPY OF EARNEST MONEY CHECK & CONTRACT FOR PURCHASE OF REAL ESTATE

❏ NAME AND ADDRESS OF INSURANCE COMPANY FOR HOMEOWNER'S/HAZARD INSURANCE

WHAT IS A LETTER OF EXPLANATION?

A letter of explanation is a short statement, written by you, that explains any derogatory or delinquent items in your credit history.

Your letter should be brief, and should explain three things:

1. Why the delinquency took place (divorce, medical bills, laid off job, or other unfortunate circumstance);

2. What you plan to do differently in the future; and

3. An acknowledgment that you understand the importance of paying your bills on time and maintaining good credit.

You must explain the following so your lender can effectively present your file for a mortgage approval:

1. Late payments (30-,60-,90-day late payments)

2. Collection Accounts

3. Judgments

4. Foreclosures

5. Bankruptcy

6. Accounts that do not belong to you (for example, if there is a car note on your credit report but someone else pays the bill with their own money from a separate account)

DON'T LET THIS SCARE YOU!!! If you have trouble, just collect your thoughts, make and outline, and your lender may help you organize this in a presentable fashion that makes sense to the underwriter.

I Do Not Have Any Credit:

How Can I Get Approved for a Mortgage?

Please obtain the following:

1. **A letter from your landlord stating that you've paid your rent on time each and every month for the time you've been renting.** If you have difficulty getting a letter from your landlord, just let him/her know that someone will call to verify your rental payment history and provide your lender your landlord's NAME, ADDRESS, AND TELEPHONE NUMBER.

2. **A letter from other creditors indicating that you have paid your accounts on time each and every month for at least the last 12 months.** The other creditors can be any of the following:

Telephone company	Gas company
Cable company	Electric company
Insurance company (life, health, auto)	Credit union loan
Cellular phone company	Pager company
Furniture company	Daycare provider
School (if you pay monthly tuition for someone)	

Try to obtain at least 4 letters to increase the likelihood of your loan application being approved.

3. If you cannot obtain a letter, a **12-month account history** is acceptable. Some companies will not send a letter, but will send an account history. Make sure a name (contact person) and telephone number are listed on any letters or account histories that you forward to your lender.

SAMPLE CEASE AND DESIST LETTER

To: COLLECTION AGENCY NAME
                 COLLECTION AGENCY ADDRESS
                 COLLECTION AGENCY CITY, STATE, ZIP
                 COLLECTION AGENCY FAX NUMBER

Attention: COLLECTION AGENT & SUPERVISOR

From: Your Name
                 Original Creditor Name
                 Original Creditor Account #

To Whom It May Concern:

You are hereby notified under provisions of Public Law 95-109, Section 805-C, The Fair Debt Collection Practices Act, to hereby CEASE AND DESIST in any and all attempts to collect the above debt. Do not call or contact the above or any of his/her immediate family members at all.

This letter is your legal notice under the above mentioned federal law that regulates the activities of collection agencies and their legal representatives.

Your failure to CEASE AND DESIST will result in charges being filed against you with the state and federal regulatory agencies empowered with the enforcement of this law.

PLEASE GIVE THIS LEGAL NOTICE YOUR FULL ATTENTION.

SAMPLE CREDIT REFERENCE LETTER

From: **Creditor Contact Person Creditor Name**
Creditor Address, City, State, Zip
Creditor Phone, Fax, Email Address

Re: **Your Name (Borrower)**   **Jane Doe**
Your Address   **123 Any Street,**
Anytown, USA 12345

Account Number	123-456-789
Account Opening Date	June 1, 2004
Account Closed Date	Currently Open
# of Times 30 Days Late	Zero times 30 days late
# of Times 60 Days Late	Zero Times 60 days late
# of Times 90+ Days Late	Zero Times 90 + days late
Current Account Status	Good Standing

To Whom It May Concern:

Please allow this letter to serve as notification of the status of the above referenced account. Please feel free to contact the undersigned if you have an questions.

Very truly yours,

Creditor Contact Person Signature

OBTAIN A COPY OF YOUR CREDIT REPORT

You are Entitled to One Free Credit Report Per Year

GET YOUR FREE ANNUAL CREDIT REPORT
www.annualcreditreport.com
877-322-8228

Or You May Order and Pay A Fee for Your Credit Reports
Directly from the Credit Reporting Agencies at Any Time:

EQUIFAX
PO Box 740241 ATLANTA, GA 30374
www.equifax.com - **800-685-1111**

EXPERIAN
PO Box 2104 ALLEN, TX 75013-2104
www.experian.com - **888-397-3742**

TRANSUNION
PO Box 2000 CHESTER, PA 19022-200
www.transunion.com – **800-888-4213**

**Most requests can be processed by calling the voice
activated system at the telephone numbers listed above.**

**Alternatively, you may process your request online
quickly and easily.**

TO: CREDIT BUREAU

FROM: Please Provide the Requestor's: Name; Current Address; Social Security Number; Date of Birth; Spouse's Name; Addresses for the Past 5 Years

IMPORTANT!!! (If the address has changed within the past 6 months, proof of current residence is included: utility bill, driver's license, etc.) – <u>Provide 2 pieces of proof</u>

Fee: (check one please)

❏ $_____ (check or money order) tax included

❏   I am eligible for a free copy of my credit report for one of the following reasons:

I have been declined credit in the past 60 days - a copy of the decline letter is attached to this letter.

I receive public assistance, a copy of my benefits card is attached.

Please mail a copy of my credit report to the current address listed above. Thank you.

Signature   Date

SAMPLE DISPUTE FORM TO SEND TO CREDIT BUREAU

Creditor	Account #

- ❏ Never Late
- ❏ Paid in Full
- ❏ Included in Bankruptcy
- ❏ Paid before Collection / Charge Off
- ❏ Account never used
- ❏ Not My Account / Other

FINAL WALK THROUGH CHECKLIST

Take your time when you are doing your final walk through inspection, which typically takes place the day before closing. Try to be as calm as possible. Many buyers have been so busy dreaming of themselves in the new home, that they neglect to take a good look and therefore miss important items that were contracted to be conveyed upon closing.

✓ If the home is being sold as-is, it may be a good idea to have your contractor or renovation consultant present to assist with measurements – remember, the Seller is leaving all repairs up to you, as stipulated in your contract.

✓ Check the house from bottom to top: basement to attic.

✓ Pay particular attention to expensive items and those that are of importance to you.

✓ Watch for areas where furniture or rugs may have been when you originally looked at the house. Many times defects in carpeting or floors that were covered are now visible.

✓ If an item is missing, or if there is trash or discarded items left behind, deal with it now. Assume that if it is gone, the sellers intend for it to be gone, or if it is still there, they do not intend to remove it.

✓ Leave your emotions outside the door. You will have plenty of time to swoon over your new home- now is the time to make sure the house is as you expected it to be.

FINAL WALK THROUGH CHECKLIST

✓   This is the time to deal with any potential problems. If you see an item that needs to be addressed, let your agent or attorney know so it can be handled *before* closing.

MOVING CHECKLIST

BEFORE YOU LEAVE YOUR CURRENT RESIDENCE:

ADDRESS CHANGE
- Post Office: Give Forwarding Address.
- Charge Accounts, Credit Cards.
- Subscriptions: Notice requires several weeks.
- Friends, Relatives.
- Real Estate, Mortgage, and Financial Consultants.

BANK
- Transfer funds, arrange check-cashing in new city.
- Arrange credit references.

INSURANCE
- Notify company of new location for coverages: Life, Health, Fire & Auto.

UTILITY COMPANIES
- Gas, light, water, telephone, cable, etc...
- Get refunds on any deposits made.

DELIVERY SERVICE
- Laundry, newspaper, milk: changeover of services.

MEDICAL, DENTAL, PRESCRIPTION HISTORIES
- Ask Doctor and Dentist for referrals.

- Transfer needed prescriptions, eyeglasses, X-rays, and obtain birth records, medical records, etc.

CHURCH, CLUB, CIVIC ORGANIZATIONS
- Transfer memberships and get letters of introduction.

MOVING CHECKLIST

PETS
- Ask about regulations for licenses, vaccinations, tags, etc.

AND DON'T FORGET TO:

- Empty freezer and plan for use or disposal of foods.
- Defrost freezer and clean refrigerator. Place charcoal to dispel odors.
- Have appliances serviced for moving.
- Remember arrangements for TV & Antenna.
- Clean rugs or clothing before moving; have them wrapped for moving.
- Check with your moving counselor: insurance coverage, packing & unpack labor, arrival day, various shipping papers, method and time of expected payment.
- Plan for special care and transportation needs of infants.

ON MOVING DAY:

- Carry enough cash or travelers checks to cover the cost of moving services and expenses and for quick available funds.

- Carry jewelry and documents yourself: or use registered mail.

- Plan for transporting pets: they are poor traveling companions if unhappy.

- Let a close friend or relative know route and schedule you will travel in moving out of town, including overnight stops: use your friend as a message headquarters.

MOVING CHECKLIST

- Double-check closets, drawers & shelves to be sure they are empty.

- Leave all old keys needed by new tenant or owner with Realtor or neighbor.

AT YOUR NEW ADDRESS:

- Obtain certified check or cashiers check necessary for closing real estate transaction.

- Check on service for telephone, gas, electricity, water, internet and cable.

- Check pilot light on stove, hot water heater, incinerator & furnace.

- Have appliances checked.

- Ask mailman for mail he/she may be holding for your arrival.

- Have new addresses recorded on driver's license.

- Visit city offices and register for voting.

- Register car within 5 days after arrival in state or a penalty may have to be paid when getting new license plates.

- Obtain inspection sticker and transfer motor club membership.

- If moving out of state, obtain a state ID and driver's license.

MOVING CHECKLIST

■   Register family in your new place of worship.

■   Arrange for medical services: Doctor, Dentist, etc.

About Lynn Richardson

"The Mortgage Guru"

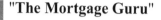

$\mathbb{K}$ nown to thousands as *"The Mortgage Guru,"* and named by Urban Influence Magazine as one of the 20 hottest influencers in America, **Lynn Richardson** is more than just another mortgage and real estate professional helping families achieve the American dream. The author, broadcaster and motivational speaker uses her quick wit and humorous presentation style to help others achieve personal, professional, and spiritual harmony. The recipient of countless awards and featured in numerous media outlets (Essence, Jet, Upscale, Tom Joyner Morning Show), **Lynn** is the Chief Operating Executive of the Hip-Hop Summit Action Network (www.hsan.org), where she works closely with co-founders Russell Simmons and Dr. Benjamin Chavis, as well as a host of A-list celebrities, to execute the organization's empowerment programs that impact the global hip-hop community.

With more than a decade of leading roles in the banking and real estate sales industries, **Lynn** became a national figure after closing more than $100 million in mortgages for urban families, most notably a lady with 4 bankruptcies and 2 foreclosures who became a homeowner after following **Lynn's** signature Mortgage Approval Plan (MAP), which is now used by industry professionals nationwide.

Lynn's industry expertise was manifested as the host of Wealth 'n Real Estate on WVON 1690am (Chicago), Vice President at American Home Mortgage, Founder of Emerging Markets Academy for Mortgage and Real Estate Professionals (where she hosts continuing education and professional development training), and Vice President of National Strategic Partnerships at JP Morgan Chase. During her tenure at Chase, **Lynn** increased outcomes by over 389% with the national Delta Sigma Theta Homeownership Initiative, where she served as National Coordinator, and she implemented the Alpha Kappa Alpha Keys to Homeownership Initiative for the world's oldest Black sorority.

Lynn expanded her influence by partnering with State Farm/Ian Smith's 50 Million Pound Challenge on the HBCU Health, Wealth 'n Real Estate Tour and she currently delivers the national real estate forecast on WVON 1690am. Her first book, Living Check to Monday, achieved Best Seller status at the 2008 Congressional Black Caucus, and the sequel, Living Beyond Check to Monday, is a powerful tool for financial and spiritual transformation.

Lynn received her undergraduate education at Northwestern University (Evanston, IL) and Loyola University Chicago and is pursuing a Master's degree in Urban Ministry at Trinity International University. She is a member of Delta Sigma Theta, Jack & Jill, the National Association of Real Estate Brokers, the National Association of Realtors, and New Faith Baptist Church. Lynn has been married to her best friend, Demietrius, for 15 years. They have 3 daughters and call a Chicago suburb home.

Lynn Richardson
. . .*the mortgage guru*

About Lori Jones Gibbs

"The People's Guru"

L ori Jones Gibbs, known as "The People's Guru," is a 25-year financial services and mortgage industry veteran. Ms. Jones Gibbs held positions with Peoples Bank, Mechanics and Farmers Bank, the North Carolina Community Development Initiative and SELF-HELP Credit Union.

Jones Gibbs is a visionary leader who created The Delta Challenge Homeownership Initiative and the Communities of Faith Home Ownership Initiative, the latter of which she partnered with Pastor and Grammy Award winning gospel legend, Shirley Caesar to spread the importance of homeownership. Currently, she is Chair of the Hip Hop Summit Action Network's National Financial Literacy Advisory Council. Jones Gibbs is a frequent speaker and panelist on issues regarding women and finances, housing policies and programming.

Jones Gibbs is currently Vice President of Affordable Housing/Industry Affairs for Genworth Mortgage Insurance. She is responsible for developing strategies to increase home ownership in diverse, under-served markets nationwide, specifically targeting low-to-moderate income, ethnic minority and New American constituencies.

Jones Gibbs serves on numerous boards, including Delta Sigma Theta Sorority's National Program Planning and Development Committee as the Economic Development Committee Chair, the Congressional Black Caucus "With Ownership Wealth" (**WOW**) National Advisory Board, HomeFree USA, Power Girls, National Bankers Association Corporate Advisory Board, North Carolina Low Income Housing Coalition, Mortgage Bankers Association Of The Carolinas and the North Carolina Council of Housing Counselors. Past board service includes immediate past National Director, Delta Sigma Theta Homeownership Initiative, City/County of Durham Merger Task Committee, the National Housing Council, St Joseph Historic Foundation and North Carolina Central University Foundation.

Honors and Awards: First African American woman to receive the Mortgage Bankers of America Diversity Champion Award, Mahogany Dime Award as One of North Carolina's Most Influential African American Women, Delta Sigma Theta Eastern Region Super Star Award, and numerous other awards.

A graduate of the University of Connecticut, Ms. Jones Gibbs holds a Masters degree from the University of Bridgeport.

Jones Gibbs is a member of First Calvary Baptist Church, Durham, NC. She is married to Kenneth Gibbs and they are the proud parents of three adult children.